John Hughes

Eagle of the Church

John Hughes
Eagle of the Church

By
Doran Hurley

Illustrated by Leonard Vosburgh

HILLSIDE EDUCATION

Hillside Education
475 Bidwell Hill Road
Lake Ariel, PA 18436
www.hillsideeducation.com

CONTENTS

1 "God Closes and Opens" 1
2 The Eagle Soars 13
3 The Young Bishop 25
4 The Schoolhouse First 41
5 American and Irish 55
6 New York's Archbishop 69
7 "Where Thy Glory Dwelleth" 87
8 Supporter of the Union 99
9 The Good Fight Ended 117
  About The Author 125

John Joseph Hughes
Eagle of the Church

1

"God Closes and Opens"

Claudit et aperit

—ARCHBISHOP HUGHES' EPISCOPAL MOTTO

After sluggish and stormy days, the battered old sailing ship welcomed wind in its sails and sun on its decks. Twenty days out from the Irish coast on the long weeks' voyage to America, it was one of the few days since sailing that the steerage hatches had been opened and the sick and weary pilgrims to the future allowed on deck. It was a poor ship and they were poor people, Irish emigrants seeking the hope and promise of a new life in a new land.

Thus far they had been treated more as cargo than as paid passengers. The baked bread and hard cakes they had brought in their chests had long since gone. There had been disputes and quarreling over sleeping space and over rights in turn to the single cooking fire. And oatmeal that was a healthy and hearty dish at home as "stirabout" was gagging aboard ship, with no exercise and too hasty cooking.

The passengers crowded to the rails now instinctively, taking great breaths of the clean sea air. Nothing was to be seen but a waste of waters, for all they hung eagerly over the rails. Still the broad blue sky and the white clouds were to them "a gift of God and the Lady Mary" after the stifling, sickening days of being herded like cattle below decks.

An old sailor coiling rope had his eye caught by a young lad as far to the bow of the ship as he was allowed to go. The youth was pressing his lithe young body urgently against the bulwarks as if to push the ship on and on by his own youthful strength.

Sailor Sullivan in his own youth had often manned the luggers that in the dark of the moon had smuggled Irish patriots from Berehaven and Dursey Island to France and Spain and priests and wine back to Bantry Bay. He remembered one young priest he had helped smuggle back whose Holy Sacrifice he had later served at the Mass Rock high up on Hungry Hill. The youth reminded him of him. He finished his coil and went up to him.

"Easy does it and far on the way." He clapped the lad on the back. "Don't strain yourself now, my lad. 'Twon't do a bit of good or I'd try it myself. It's been a slow voyage and bad. But now, St. Brendan and good winds, that's all we need. Say a good prayer to the one for the other. That's a deal better than trying to push the ship by your lea-lone."

John Hughes turned quickly, then grinned. The old and grizzled West Cork sailor had used the Gaelic "ma gossoon" in calling him "my lad." It gave him friendly kinship. But his thoughts had been so intense that he continued them in his speech for all his friendly grin.

"I am afloat on this ocean, looking for a home and a country in which no stigma of inferiority will be impressed on my brow simply because I expressed one creed or another."

"Do you tell me now?" said the sailor, not a bit taken aback since his own thoughts had been of the young priest in the mountain dawn. "Well, you're a lad of spirit anyway, but I could see that from the first. You'll make out. And I don't think I'd care to be the one to cross you once you had your mind made. You're from the North by your way of talking but the rebel's in you for all that. What special is on your mind now you want to get to America so fast and determined?"

His voice was kindly and understanding and the Cork lilt came gently. John Hughes had found no congenial friend below decks. The lack of cleanliness from the unfortunate people who were ill and the fretful squabbling about cooking rights had lowered his spirits. He had drawn into himself. Now, for all his natural reserve, he felt deeply that he must pour out his heart to someone.

In a burst of speech he told the gnarled old man that he was from County Tyrone, born in the village of Annaloghan on St. John's Day, June 24, in 1797. It had once been O'Neill's land, Hugh O'Neill, Earl of Tyrone. Now it was a land of Scottish "planters"; and the Old Faith and the people who shared it were bitterly persecuted.

The sailor's hand moved up to rest on his shoulder. To prove his understanding he said that he, himself, was of the Clan O'Sullivan, of the O'Sullivan Bere, Lord of Bere and Bantry, who had been the great O'Neill's friend.

John Hughes told his own new friend that he was the third of seven children of Patrick Hughes and Margaret McKenna. His father had been a stout farmer who could have made out well had he not been a devout Catholic in an Orange, or Protestant, community where the Irish penal laws rode heavily on the people.

"Once as a boy, I was returning from a peaceable night errand for my Da when I was stopped on the road by a band of five Orangemen and five bayonets thrust at my breast. It was only when one man, a near neighbor, recognized me as my father's son that I was allowed to go on without harm. And I was only a boy. Had I been older I might well have been cruelly beaten for no reason at all save that I was Catholic. Yet always my father took no sides, but tried only to live at peace with the neighbors, bearing no one any hate or ill will."

"I know, I know well." The sailor tightened his grip on John's shoulder. "It is why I took to the sea in earnest when my old people died and no longer needed me to shield them."

"But worst of all, and it nearly broke my mother's heart," John continued with tight lips, "was when tiny little sister died. There was a priest in the neighborhood at the time and we got word to him. There was no question of a Mass but someone guessed who he was and he was not even let enter the burying ground to bless her grave. It was then I knew as surely as if God Himself had told me that for the saving of my own soul I must leave Ireland."

More quietly he told of his schooling at Augher and later at Aughnaclory, walking miles to get the little education available. He had studied from odd books when he worked on his father's farm holdings away from the homestead. Then he had hired himself out to the head gardener of the Montray family whose great estate was nearby. That, too, gave him a chance to improve himself.

"They praised my green thumbs," he said pridefully, then ruefully, "even if they hated the green I wore in my heart but couldn't wear in my cap."

His father and his elder brother, Patrick, had given up the unequal struggle and sailed for America a year before. Now he was joining them so that with his work and wages they might more quickly bring his mother and the rest of the family to America's free land.

"Then maybe when that is a done thing," he said, now somewhat shyly, "the time may come and the way will be opened for me to realize the one dream I have in life for my own self—a dream I hold with my whole heart and soul and which my mother shares with me."

"God guide your hand and your heart," said the Sailor Sullivan gruffly, "for I have a mind your dream is no selfish one. God and Mary bless it and you."

"Oh, they will. They will! I know it so surely. No matter what striving lies ahead." The youth's tone was buoyant with belief. "For many a time have I thrown down my rake in the meadow and kneeling behind a haystack begged God and the Blessed Virgin to let me become . . . a *priest!*"

It was in 1817 that John Hughes saw for the first time the free land he was so to love and proudly to serve. He went first to Baltimore after he landed. His brother Patrick had found work outside the city. John's first job was assisting the gardener of a nursery on Maryland's Eastern Shore. He plunged into the work eagerly. It was what he felt best suited to do. But the job was only temporary. The coming of winter brought it to an end.

He joined his father at Chambersburg, Pennsylvania. Work of his liking was hard to find, but work of any kind he was glad to do. He was young and strong and his immediate objective was to help his father raise as quickly as possible the moneys needed to send for his mother and sisters. He gladly went as a laborer to help build a millrace and a bridge a little distance from Chambersburg.

He boarded while the work went on with a teacher, Master Mullan, who was of the same period and devotion to scholarship as Abraham Lincoln's first teacher, Master Zachariah Riney.

Master Mullan used to jest with John that it was London Bridge he was building, and that the attic room the youth rented was London Tower.

"Take your books and your candle to the Tower. And away with you," he would say after John had eaten his evening meal. It warmed Master Mullan's heart to find a strapping, vigorous youth eager for books and reading rather than sports or idling. He pressed his own books on John eagerly.

More than that, he sent word to the priest who as a "saddlebag missionary" rode through the area that he had a promising young scholar staying with him. Samuel Cooper was the first American priest John Hughes knew well. Mr. Cooper (for the term Father was not yet in use) took great interest in John. He helped him with the Latin he was studying under Master Mullan's guidance, correcting the old schoolmaster's honest errors in self-taught grammar and pronunciation. He encouraged John to begin the study of Greek. He lent him minor theological works by Bishop Richard Challoner from his own small store. When Mass was said at Master Mullan's house or at a walkable distance in miles, John served Mr. Cooper as acolyte and reported on his studies.

Chambersburg was only thirty miles from Emmitsburg in Maryland. There, hardly ten years before, Father John Dubois, an exile from France, had established Mount

St. Mary's College, the first United States seminary for the training of priests. It was a poor and struggling college.

John's little savings had gone regularly to his father. With his and Patrick's help at last in 1818 the passage money was sent to Ireland to his mother and sisters and the family was reunited.

The reunion was joyous and blessed. But after the early excitement was over John's mother took him aside.

"Are you holding fast to your dream, my son?" she asked. "It is the thing most often in my prayers."

Her eyes lightened when he told her of his studies with Mr. Cooper and Master Mullan. Because they shared the dream now, he felt free to tell her that he had tried with their encouragement to be taken as a student at Mount St. Mary's College once the journey money for the rest of the family had been raised.

"The fees are small but I could see no way to pay them. And it's not as if it were a rich college. The money is needed just so it can keep going. They were right to refuse me. I'd only be a burden—for the only thing I had to offer was my hands."

"Your hands—of course, your hands! Your green hands, John, that make God's green things grow so richly. Did you tell them how you worked for the Montrays and how the gardener gave praise to your face, that dour man? And the job of work in the gardens you had here at first? No! I thought not. It is only as a laborer they think of you who have beguiled the priest and the Master.

"They grow their own food or much of it at this priest school, you tell me. Go again to them and tell them that you will work in their gardens and orchards for even half schooling. Show them, on trial, how God's things grow for you. God gave you those hands, John!

Young John Hughes flung himself into the task of making the college garden flourish.

Offer them to study in His service. We've no need more now of your help. Just bring those hands back to me—blessed."

Father John Dubois listened gently as was his wont to the new pleading of this so earnest young man. "So earnest— so American in his vigor," he commented to himself, "even though he is not long here. It is wrong to give him hope; he is as yet not well-schooled and of an intellectual crudeness. But it might be more wrong to send him away."

He told John finally that he could give him a post tending the college gardens but could pay him little more than his board and keep. He could hold out little hope that it would be possible for John to attend classes. Perhaps, but he could give no promises.

It was all John and his mother had prayed might happen. To John it was a blessed ray piercing the clouds. He startled Father Dubois by asking if he might get to work at once— there were still several hours until sundown.

He flung himself into the task of making the college garden flourish with a vigor that at first irked the other workers, Timothy and Peter, that he had to help him with the heavier work. Even had he thought of such a thing, the job would have held no humiliation for John; for everyone, faculty and students alike, did some work with their hands at the struggling Mount St. Mary's.

His training in Ireland and those green thumbs stood him in good stead. He added to the size of the vegetable patch and planted different varieties. He pruned the apple and pear and peach trees as he had been taught, so they bore richer fruit. The sparse meals in the college refectory grew in wholesomeness and appeal. The delighted students now often offered to help John in little ways in their free time. He was generous with an apple or a bunch of grapes.

Even gentle Father Dubois, who rarely knew what he was eating, began to notice that his appetite was growing and that he did not mind nearly so much having his work interrupted to be called to the table. One day he tucked up his cassock when the thought struck him and made his way out to the farm lands to tell John how pleased he was. It was in the brief time at noon that the lad snatched for his own dinner. Timothy and Peter were sleeping, but John he found under a tree deep in study, his packaged meal beside him untouched.

The volume he was scanning earnestly with a pointed finger was *The Confessions of St. Augustine*—and in Latin. It was far beyond the learning Father John Dubois thought John had. He had him read an early passage in translation. It was well and freely done.

The priest was not given to quick decisions; but he made one then, on the spot, in the orchard. "You are not wasted in the work you are doing here. I came to tell you that. Your hands are not wasted nor your body. And I see you are not letting your mind go to waste. But perhaps, God help me, I am helping waste your soul. If you will oversee this work in your own time, if you can do that, come to me tonight when work is ended. I shall enroll you as a student and examine you to see what class you might enter." John Hughes was then twenty-six.

Of all his studies at Mount St. Mary's, the closest to John's heart were the classes in theology under Father Simon Brute, who was to become the great pioneer Bishop of the western frontier, as John Dubois became Bishop of New York. And it was through Father Brute that John came to know and admire Mother Seton, the foundress of the Sisters of Charity in the United States, who had established her convent at Emmitsburg. At that time Father Brute was her spiritual adviser and staunch friend.

The students at the college accepted John Hughes as a fellow collegian and closer companion readily and joyously. For all his usual seriousness, he could when he willed become a gay companion, with a fund of Irish ballads that he could be coaxed to sing. And soon he became the college hero.

A forest fire started on the mountain above the school lands. It flared through the brush and quickly threatened the college buildings. The alarm was sudden. It was study hour. John was bent over his desk in his best black coat. He liked to emphasize by his dress in what capacity he was acting, gardener or student. Unheeding, he rushed out with the others when the alarm was sounded.

He quickly took command of the fire fighters, deploying priests and boys to the best advantage. He had them stamp the unburned brush down and beat at the crawling flames with wet sacks. He organized a bucket brigade from the college well. With Peter and Timothy, loyal beside him, he was at the front of the fight. And his was the victory—but it left its mark.

As he turned away from the fire, a burst of flying sparks burned a great hole across the shoulders of his coat. He did not notice it until Peter bravely kept slapping at him. Back at the college, he ruefully sewed on a patch that he thought was nearest like the original cloth. It was no match at all, but no student laughed at it. Father Dubois set the example. He embraced John and thanked him. Then holding him off with his back to the assembled school, he called the patch "our dear boy's badge of honor."

John Hughes spent seven years at the college, happily combining his work and studies. In time he had advanced so far scholastically that he was made instructor to the beginning classes. That helped even more than his supervision of the gardens to pay for his own continuing education. Later he was to say proudly, "I never received of the charity of any man; I never borrowed of any man without repaying; I never had more than a few dollars at a time; I never had a patron in the Church or out of it." That spirit of fierce independence— that of the eagle that is the symbol alike of St. John the Evangelist for whom he was named and the United States of his adoption—grew on him early and never left him.

In 1825 he was ordained deacon. In that year, in a sense, he entered the active ministry. He was invited by Bishop Henry Conwell to whom Fathers Dubois and Brute had recommended him, to accompany him on an episcopal visitation. Without warning he found the Bishop expected him to preach. It amused the Bishop that in six different places he heard Deacon John preach the same sermon. It was the only one he had prepared and there was no chance to ready another. John's "cuckoo sermon," the Bishop teasingly called it, reminding him that the cuckoo, of all birds, repeats the same note over and over again.

Then at last came the fulfilment of the dream, God's answer to the prayers that first went up in the hayfields of Ireland. John Hughes was ordained a priest. It was October 15, 1826, the Feast of St. Teresa of Avila. Bishop Conwell was the ordaining prelate in St. Joseph's Church, Philadelphia.

"Blessed be God. Blessed be His Holy Name," whispered Mary McKenna Hughes as her son John's consecrated hands descended on her head in blessing.

2

THE EAGLE SOARS

Gentle when stroked, fierce when provoked
—SLOGAN OF IRISH SIXTY-NINTH NEW YORK REGIMENT

The church of Father John Hughes' ordination soon became that of his first full pastorate. He was the most vigorous shepherd of his flock that St. Joseph's or later, St. Mary's, in placid Philadelphia had ever known. In the general life of the Quaker City, Catholic priests had obeyed the precept laid down for well- mannered children—of being seen but not heard.

Father Hughes changed all that. Not only his parishioners but the non-Catholic citizens of Philadelphia soon found that he was an Irishman of the wolfhound breed, ready to spring forth on any and all occasions as a bold defender of his Faith. If the city's dedication was truly to Brotherly Love, then Father John Hughes was going to fight for his own people's share of it.

Surprisingly his very aggressiveness won friends and even many converts from the Society of Friends, the Quakers or Plain People. Father Hughes found somewhat less satisfaction in his dealings with his own parishioners. He found many of them sadly lacking in the simple unquestioning faith and ardent devotion of the Catholics of his Irish boyhood.

He wrote of them rather tartly in a letter to his sister Ellen—now Sister Mary Angela of Mother Seton's Sisters of Charity. In telling her of his parish work among them and also, proudly, of his steadily growing number of converts, he said wryly:

"If the Catholics themselves were what they should be, the number of converts would be astonishing."

He devoted himself fiercely to seeing that the Catholics under his charge *were* what they should be, insofar as it was in his priestly power. He wanted neither second-class Catholics nor second-class citizens. He carried his Catholic Americanism like a banner, holding it aloft for all men to see and recognize. It was cold comfort that his tongue gave some of his more lax parishioners when he encountered them on his rounds as he tramped through the parish streets and lanes swinging his blackthorn stick.

"You were late for Mass last Sunday, James Fogarty. . . . You've drink taken again I see, Patrick Barry. . . . Fine example you are to the neighbors, Julia Brown—I heard your bold tongue wagging ten doorsteps away. . . . Move on now, you lads, away from that corner trying to ogle the girls! Move on, I say, or I'll have the watch onto you. . . ."

He knew that he was too often impatient and headstrong and apt in anger to lack charity. He tried hard to control his impetuousness and rash judgments; but it was not easy as he confessed in his letters to Father Brute. He turned always and frequently to the elder priest for spiritual counseling. Under Father Brute's direction he turned the surplus energy that was always his into deeper studies in theology and apologetics.

Rather plaintively once, in answer to a question from Father Brute that touched his pride as an unfair scolding, he wrote his old teacher: "Parties of pleasure are *not* frequented by me, and except one, I am sure I visit less than any clergyman in the city."

He meant, of course, purely social visits; for he was tireless in calling at the homes of his parishioners, particularly if they were ill or in need. At the same time, for all his protestations, he was in great demand in the city as a dinner guest. He was considered a great wit when he was in good form and some of his sallies were widely quoted. And when he was very sure of his company he sometimes could be prevailed upon to sing an Irish ballad in his deep bass-baritone. The rebel songs: "The Wearin' of the Green" and "The Croppy Boy" were two of his favorites.

Very early as a parish priest he began to take up his writing cudgel against those he considered defamers of the Catholic Church. A widely circulated pamphlet of the day purported to tell of "The Conversion and Edifying Death of Andrew Dunn." The very fictional Andrew was supposedly a Catholic Irishman who saw the error of his Papist ways and died an Orangeman. Somehow Father Hughes got hold of a copy of the pamphlet and it infuriated him. He immediately sat down and wrote a counter-story. It was not an inspired work, for to have Father Hughes' story make sense you would have needed to have read the original. But he was so pleased with his effort after he had re-read it that he had it published in pamphlet form, also.

In another writing instance as defender of the Faith, Father John allowed himself a bit of waggish fun. A newspaper called *The Protestant* had been publishing a series of misstatements about the Church. In a burst of Irish mischief, John Hughes decided to go the editor one better.

Signing himself "Crammer," he wrote a long letter telling with assumed horror of the terrible inroads of the Papists into hitherto pure Pennsylvania. In Philadelphia he wrote, there were no less than "four Mass houses made to hold twelve congregations . . . with an extra Mass late in the afternoon."

There was, of course, no such thing as an afternoon or evening Mass then. Nor was there any "suspicious nunnery" or convent of any kind in Cambria County, Pennsylvania, or Jesuit College in Pittsburgh, although "Crammer" described them in awful detail.

But great was Father Hughes' glee when *The Protestant* published his letter-parody in full, with the editor adding a note that "Our Philadelphia friend communicates his melancholy intelligence in a very evangelical spirit of sensibility and fervour."

In his various parish pulpits Father Hughes had steadily made progress as a preacher since the days of his first lame "cuckoo sermon." His talks were sound in doctrine but on the whole disappointing to congregations that rated a preacher by the fire and fury of his oratory. John Hughes laid down "the law and the prophets" but he did it in a cold factual way. Because he thought his people needed most to have the Gospels explained to them in simple, practical language he never let himself go in the impassioned eloquence of the great preachers of the day.

A sermon he delivered on May 31, 1829, changed all that. Several weeks before, King George IV of England had signed the bill emancipating English Catholics from the laws that discriminated against them. The Catholics of Philadelphia were eager to join the rejoicing of their kinsmen over the water. Old St. Augustine's Church, to the building of which George Washington and Commodore John Barry had contributed large sums, was chosen for the solemn Mass of Thanksgiving.

Father Michael Hurley, an Augustinian friar and a close friend of Mother Seton, was pastor of the historic church. It was expected that he would preach the sermon, since his fame was great as a pulpit orator and men and women from all over the city would be on hand for the thanksgiving service.

Instead Father Hurley chose to be celebrant of the Mass, and to the surprise of many picked Father John Hughes to preach the sermon. In the first years of his priesthood Father John had served Father Michael as an earnest young curate. The older priest knew the inner fire of his spirit. He also knew how deeply the signing of the Catholic Emancipation Bill affected John, who had known personal suffering in his boyhood from the restrictions that the statute now removed. He decided to give the younger priest his great chance.

"Push aside the books on your table, John. Forget them when you take up your pen. Use your good mind, of course, but for this one time let your heart rule it. The people will expect it. Let yourself go, John! Invite us to lift up our hearts and sing. Make us rejoice, John! Peal out to us the glad tidings! But why should I talk? I know well you'll not fail me."

For once John Hughes was truly humble. "Father Michael," he said in a surge of emotion, "I shall call unceasingly upon the Holy Spirit that He may quicken me. If I somehow succeed, you and I will know it is only because the Third Person of the Blessed Trinity has answered my prayers."

Long before the solemn Mass was to start, the church was crowded beyond its capacity and hundreds of devout people gathered in the streets outside. The huge congregation fell to a great hush when, at the Gospel, Father John Hughes in surplice and preaching stole ascended the pulpit. The hush went forth from the church to the massed crowds outside.

He chose his text from the 84th Psalm: "Lord, thou hast blessed thy land: thou hast turned away the captivity of Jacob. . . . Mercy and truth have met each other: justice and peace have kissed. Truth is sprung out of the earth: and justice hath looked down from heaven."

John Hughes' pulpit voice has been described as "clear, sonorous and tenderly sympathetic." It was totally unlike his conversational gruffness at times. Up to now he had used its natural musical richness sparingly. Now he let it go forth as if he were playing upon a great cathedral organ. Its richness matched the unusual eloquence of his poetical language.

Old priests crowded together in the sanctuary poked and prodded each other in open admiration as one glowing sentence after another rang through the church.

"Dear me, I never expected it," whispered one elderly Father to the priest jammed next to him. "Bless my soul, this day he's another Saint Paul."

"No, no, no, begging your pardon, Father. Its John he was rightly christened. The eagle is the symbol of St. John. Like the eagle, John Hughes will soar high. He shows every sign now of becoming in God's time our own great and proud American Catholic eagle."

Those standing at the crowded back of the church kept

shouting behind them to the people in the streets the stirring phrases of the great sermon. The people closest re-echoed them and passed them on. It was odd in the silence of the church to hear cheers outside as a telling bit of eloquent speech found kinship in the people's hearts.

So tremendous was the impact of the Emancipation sermon upon the congregation at St. Augustine's that those who caught it only in bits and pieces wanted a chance to read and thrill to it for themselves. It was put into pamphlet form by insistent popular demand. It circulated widely throughout every Catholic community in the United States and scores of copies were sent abroad to friends in England and Ireland. That one stirringly magnificent sermon made John Hughes almost at once an important national Catholic figure.

The published version John Hughes dedicated to the great Irish leader who was then and always one of his great personal heroes: "To the man who is at once the Scholar, the Patriot, the consistent Christian, and the practical Catholic, Daniel O'Connell, Esq. . . so rare a combination in a public character."

The compliments that began to come John Hughes' way did not turn his head in the least. He continued on his parochial way. In that same year all his extra energies went toward the establishment of a Catholic orphan asylum, St. John's.

He brushed aside all talk that came to him that the aging and ailing Bishop Conwell, who was giving up the active administration of the diocese, was pressing his name on Rome as coadjutor bishop with right of succession. Bishop Conwell had been parish priest of Dungannon in John Hughes' own county of Tyrone before he had been made

Bishop of Philadelphia. This had been an extra bond between them, but John Hughes was too proudly independent to trespass on that.

When Bishop Francis Patrick Kenrick was named in 1830 to succeed Bishop Conwell, John Hughes was closely watched for signs of disappointment. By now Father Hughes was acknowledgedly the leading Catholic priest of the city. Surely it would go hard for him to work with and take orders from a man close to his own age and a stranger to the city!

But John Hughes and Bishop Kenrick became the closest of friends and associates. Father John soon became the Bishop's secretary and right-hand man. It was he who at the Bishop's instance built the new church, dedicated in 1832, that was later to become Philadelphia's Catholic cathedral. It was named after John's own patron, St. John the Evangelist— the saint whose symbol is the eagle.

The Catholic people of Philadelphia, save for a few like Mathew Carey, the publisher—"honest Mat Carey of Phil"— were very poor. The parishes under the "trustee system," or lay control of church property, were laden with debts. At one time John Hughes began the study of Spanish. He had an idea that if he were skilled enough in the language, and the Bishop gave his permission, he would try to finance a trip to Mexico and beg for help for the Philadelphia Church from wealthy Catholics there. In the meantime he went about the various parishes under his administration, a zealous pastor encouraging and sometimes scolding, but always watchful of the welfare of his. flock.

In 1832, Philadelphia was swept by the terrible scourge of the Asiatic cholera. Cholera is a pestilence of cruelly nauseating and revolting symptoms. In those days it was as often fatal as not. As always happened when such plagues struck, the wealthy fled the city. Among the poor, crowded together in their poverty, death went from family to family.

Bishop Kenrick threw all the possible resources of the Church into the fight to aid and save Catholics and non-Catholics alike. He turned the parish buildings of St. Augustine's into a temporary hospital. He made John Hughes his commander in the field, and Father John was tireless. He was as scornful of danger as he had been when he led the boy fire fighters at Mount St. Mary's.

The Bishop had released the Sisters of Charity from all other duties that they might tend the sick under Father John's leadership. The Mayor and Corporation of Philadelphia were so grateful to the nuns for the inspired, healing work they accomplished during the Philadelphia cholera epidemic that, when it was over, without a dissenting vote, His Honor and the Aldermen gallantly and gratefully tendered the Sisters "a service of plate."

The Sisters, through Father John, politely declined the gift. "They are dedicated to God, that's why," he bluntly told the Mayor when he was questioned about it. "They live by the great commandments: to love thy God and thy neighbor as thyself. Don't you know about the corporal works of mercy, to visit the sick and bury the dead? That's all they did, these good women, put into active work among you and for you the principle on which Penn is said to have founded our city—the principle of Brotherly Love."

Then came another unsolicited happening that projected John Hughes again into an even wider national prominence. It was a challenge to a written debate by one of the most noted Protestant clergymen of the day, the Reverend

John Breckenridge, who stood high in the councils of the Presbyterian Church.

Father Hughes, who had recently established a diocesan newspaper, *The Catholic Herald,* and become its editor, eagerly accepted the challenge. For several months the debate, with rebuttals and counterrebuttals, was carried on between him and Mr. Breckenridge in the secular Philadelphia journals and excited great and unusual interest.

In the end, of course, neither man had made a convert of the other. But it was the sort of intellectual exercise in which Father Hughes delighted. Interest in the controversy was so keen that pamphlets covering the whole debate were issued and had wide circulation far beyond Philadelphia. It was the general opinion that, take it all in all and to be fair, the Catholic priest did seem to have a bit the better of the argument.

Philadelphia was swept by the terrible scourge of the Asiatic cholera.

The Reverend Mr. Breckenridge acknowledgedly lost face. He remained silent for four years; then egged on by some of his supporters he issued a second challenge for debate on the question: "Is the Roman Catholic Religion, in any and all of its principles and doctrines, inimical to civil or religious liberty?" This new question gave Father Hughes a glorious chance to show that Catholicism was completely hospitable and friendly to the civil and religious liberties of the still young nation.

Theologically he could call upon the name of the Jesuit Cardinal Bellarmine, so many of whose moral and ethical judgments had been woven into the fabric of the Constitution. Historically he could point to Charles Carroll of Carrollton, the signer of the Declaration of Independence, whose death the whole nation had mourned just two years before. He could

refer to the choice by the Congress of Bishop John Carroll to accompany Benjamin Franklin in the delegation that hoped to win Canada to the Revolutionary cause. He could cite the many instances, so well known to Philadelphians, when President George Washington had publicly shown how deeply he appreciated the aid of his fellow Catholic citizens in the cause of liberty.

The articles in the second debate were published in book form soon after it was over. The book had a tremendous circulation, but it was generally conceded that it was Father John Hughes' book and not his opponent's. John Hughes' name swept out of Philadelphia northward to Boston, southward to Maryland and Virginia and the Carolinas, westward to the Kentucky frontier and down the Mississippi to New Orleans.

The onetime poor young Irish emigrant gardener now belonged to no single parish or city or diocese. The Catholic people of the whole nation claimed him, with approving pride in his stalwart Americanism. The eagle began to lift his strong wings.

3

THE YOUNG BISHOP

Ad Multos Annos! (For many years!)
—WORDS CHANTED AT THE CONSECRATION OF A BISHOP

Father Hughes' old teacher and friend, now Bishop John Dubois of New York, had become enfeebled. Through age and illness he could no longer adequately shepherd the people of his fast-growing diocese. In 1837 he wrote to Rome to the Holy Father, Pope Gregory XVI, asking that he be granted an assistant bishop. On the recommendation of the other American Bishops and at Bishop Dubois' own warm plea, Pope Gregory raised John Hughes to the post and rank of coadjutor, with the right of succession.

Inwardly John Hughes shrank from the new responsibilities. He had never thought of himself as a particularly good administrator. He had worked well and closely with Bishop Kenrick in the governing of the Philadelphia see; but for all that he still felt that in study and writing lay his true apostolate.

His name, it is true, had once been mentioned as bishop coadjutor to Bishop Conwell. He had been strongly considered for the vacant see of Cincinnati. But he had successfully begged off from the dignity and advancement then.

In his direct way he commented at that time, "I had studied the inside as well as the outside of a mitre, and I regarded him who is obliged to wear it as entitled to pity, not envy."

But his love for his old teacher and his deep loyalty to him was so great that now he set his own wishes aside. He could not hold back from helping in his age the man who had so helped him toward the burning dream of his youth—the sacred priesthood.

John Hughes was consecrated as coadjutor of New York, under the title of Bishop of Basileopolis, January 7, 1838, in the first St. Patrick's Cathedral on Mott Street in lower New York City. Bishop Dubois presided at the liturgical imposition of hands. Bishop Kenrick of Philadelphia and Bishop Benedict Fenwick of Boston were the co-consecrators. The Jesuit Father Mulledy of Georgetown University preached the sermon.

There were enthusiasm and joy among the Catholics of New York over the appointment of John Hughes. Try as he would, they had held themselves apart from Bishop Dubois, so very French in his ways. Many times he had been made to feel he was tending alien corn. But everyone knew all about Father John Hughes, an American priest, of the blood of most of them.

So great was the clamoring for pew seats for the consecration ceremonies that even before the Bishop-elect had reached New York, the cathedral authorities began to build tall and broad platforms over the graves in the churchyard. These were designed so that those who could not possibly squeeze into the church or find room on the steps at the opened doors might be able to get glimpses of the solemn ceremonies and hear the preacher through the open windows.

John Hughes looked forward to an association similar to that he had had with Bishop Kenrick. He would work himself into his new duties gradually. There would be long and affectionate talks at night and wise and gentle counseling as he learned his duties and his way.

Within two weeks of his consecration he had to bear the whole burden of administering the vast diocese. Two successive paralytic attacks made the elder Bishop a helpless invalid.

The see of New York at that time comprised the whole state of New York and about half of New Jersey. The Catholic population numbered about 200,000 souls, with forty priests and twenty churches. Fifteen priests labored in eight parishes on the island of Manhattan. Schools were few. Only in New York City and Albany were they little more than church-basement catechism classes. Mother Seton's daughters had barely been able to make the beginnings of their great teaching work.

Perhaps a little wistfully Bishop Hughes put aside his books and his studies. He plunged into the practical work of the far-flung diocese with the same vigor that had marked his parish work, his building of churches and an orphanage in Philadelphia, and his written debates in defense of the Church. He set out at once on an episcopal visitation.

He was away from the city when word came to him in 1839 that he had been named full administrator of the diocese. Bishop Dubois' incapabilities had increased. Bishop

Hughes was then on a whirlwind visitation of northern New York where the Catholics had suffered some neglect. He rode like a circuit preacher from hamlet to hamlet, catechizing, confirming, and giving sermon after sermon.

In Onondaga County his questing zeal for souls unearthed a Catholic colony of sixteen all of whom were converts, although there was no priest stationed nearer than forty miles.

"Never thought as how I'd ever meet a real Bishop," the tall, lanky farmer who was the spokesman of the group said shyly and awkwardly to John Hughes. "Don't get to see a priest real often but we do the best we can holding on to the Faith. Your coming all the way up this way means a lot to us. Encourages us a lot. Almost as good as seeing the Pope, in a way. But we could never talk to him as real easy as we can to you. You're a mighty plain-spoken man."

"But tell me, so far away from a church or a priest— beside the grace of the good God what led you all into the Church in the first place?"

"Well," said the farmer pulling at his ear a little bashfully, "it was this way. Fellow came through selling little books. Pack on his back. Come along toward nighttime. We're kind of out of the way so we put him up for the night. Weren't much interested in books he had to sell. Didn't seem to fit in with our way of thinking. But the man himself kind of took with us.

"Religious sort of fellow outside but you could see he was real good inside, too. Got to talking after supper and he knew his Bible. Certainly did. And when a point come up he would pick up one of his books and read out the answer. Sounded good. The real God's truth. Got him to stay on a few days. Talked some more. Made no bones about being a Papist. Just didn't seem to bother us. Well, guess in a way it did. Set us thinking. Upshot was he left some of his books with us. We kind of studied them over, one and another. Decided us. Finally got word to nearest town with a priest. Well, there we were—and here we are!"

As full administrator of the diocese, Bishop Hughes soon realized that he needed to raise money to carry on its affairs. His people were rich in faith but poor in purse. His trips outside the city to upstate New York and to New Jersey showed the dire need of mission churches and more priests. A seminary for the training of priests was one of the greatest needs. After long thought, he decided to humble himself and go on a begging trip to the rich Catholic countries of Europe. He sailed for Le Havre, France, October 16, 1839, in the packet *Louis Philippe*.

His air of earnest authority and dignity quickly made him friends in high places. In Paris, the American Ambassador, General Lewis Cass, was delighted to find no uncouth backwoods bishop but an urbane and polished gentleman. He excitedly offered to present John Hughes to King Louis Philippe.

"Of course," the Ambassador said, "His Majesty prides himself on being what he calls 'the Citizen King.' But still he really doesn't like people to presume on that. At odd moments he is apt to remember that he is not only a king but that he is sprung from kings," he added anxiously.

John Hughes gave him a sudden big grin. "They do say that all we Irish are sprung from kings; and that those who didn't spring from them sprang *at* them. But I'll mind my manners, you may be sure. After all," he said gently, "I *am* of a land where every man as a citizen is equally a king."

Louis Philippe was delighted to meet John Hughes.

The French King went out of his way to be cordial to the American Bishop, especially when he learned that he had passed so many years as a priest in Philadelphia. From 1796 to 1800, when he was in exile from France after the French Revolution, Louis had lived in that city with his two brothers. It was a little before John Hughes' time, but still there was much they had in common about people and places there.

"Tell me, Lord Bishop," said the King at one point, "is it true what is told me by the Count de Tocqueville, who at a later time was able to go more deeply into things than I? Alexis says that in Boston he heard it said that 'The Catholics always vote for the most democratic party . . . and that Baltimore, where they predominate, is the most democratic town in the Union.'"

"No one is more deeply American than our Catholic people," John Hughes answered sturdily, "nor closer to our democratic principles. Each of us is an equal citizen. Each of us is, in his own right, a king who never fears to lose his throne." Louis laughed loudly at the Bishop's sally, but some of the courtiers present looked uneasy.

In Rome, Pope Gregory XVI opened his arms warmly to his American son. The Holy Father was a man of many sorrows because of the European revolutions which had even invaded his own Papal States. He was happy to honor a bishop of a country where the Catholic Church was growing in respect and in dignity. From his impoverished treasury he could offer John Hughes little money, but he heaped honors upon him and gave him personal presents of vestments and church vessels, chalices and monstrances and crucifixes.

John Hughes passed three months in Rome on his begging mission. It was a joy to him to visit the great churches of the ancient city and within his priestly heart grew another dream.

It was an impossible dream for a beggar bishop to have—but no more impossible, he felt, than the dream of the Irish farm boy as he knelt and prayed behind the haystacks.

One of the churches he visited most often was that of San Pietro di Montorio where the last of the Irish earls, Hugh O'Neill of Tyrone and Hugh O'Donnell of Tyrconnel, were buried. He liked to think that he had a special link to the two great Hughs, since his own name in the Gaelic would be MacHugh or son of Hugh.

On the last day of his stay in Rome, he made a special trip to the tombs of the great Irish earls and said a special rosary.

"St. Patrick," he prayed, "look kindly on this new dream I have just as Our Lord and Our Lady blessed the dream of my boyhood. Bishop Patrick, I preside over the faithful in a great city dedicated to you. My people, yours and mine, are only poor laborers and servant girls; but they have generous hearts anxious to do you honor. Inspire these O'Neills and O'Donnells, these Sullivans and Murphys and McCarthys, to help me, even if all they can give are pennies, to build a great cathedral as fine as any in these old lands of Europe where your name may be blessed for generations."

Pope Gregory sent John on to Vienna with his blessings, hopeful he might enlist the aid of the Leopoldine Society which had been organized in 1829 for the promotion of missions in America. It was named after the Archduchess Leopoldina, Empress of Brazil.

In Vienna, Bishop Hughes again proved his adaptability to court life. He charmed the nobles of the Austrian court. His task was made the easier because in high places were many descendants of old Irish families who had left Ireland as "Wild Geese," as these exiles were called.

The Leopoldine Society gave the American Bishop a large

donation for the college and seminary for the training of priests that he proposed to build in the countryside to the north of New York City. An earlier rude seminary, St. Vincent de Paul's, had been started much too far away from the city to enlist students. It had been at a place called Lafargeville for the forebears of a family to become noted in the annals of the Catholic Church in America.

The site that Bishop Hughes had in mind for the new college of St. John was also considered by many to be a bit out of the way—an estate known as Rose Hill Farm. It was admitted, however, that boys studying for the priesthood should live and be taught well apart from the city's distractions. Rose Hill in its isolation was satisfactory in that respect. It was then a long, long journey from town away up to Fordham where it was situated.

On his way home, London gave Bishop Hughes a dignified reception, Dublin an enthusiastic one. His greatest joy was in meeting at last his cherished hero, Daniel O'Connell, who after Catholic Emancipation bore the title of "The Liberator."

His European begging trip had been successful. He returned with art treasures for the churches and with the money he needed to start his seminary and to help straighten out the tangled finances of the diocese. He felt encouraged to go forward with plans for the future growth of his see.

On the 20th of December, 1842, Bishop John Dubois died. John Hughes assumed the full dignity of Bishop of New York. He was then forty-five years of age, and he himself was not in the best of health; for although his spirit had the vigor of old he had driven himself too hard.

Earlier in that year, on another of his whirlwind visitations of parishes in the north and west of the state, his schedule was backbreaking even for a younger man of his day. "I arrived in Binghamton late on a Saturday night," he wrote at that time. "The next day I administered Confirmation, preached four times and dedicated a new church. On Monday I preached twice and dedicated a graveyard. Tuesday I rode thirty miles to Oxford, New York, preached and left the same evening for Utica. . . ." This was but a sample of his rounds for weeks on end, in good weather and bad, traveling in springless buggies on primitive roads, with eating and sleeping accommodations often poor.

Back in New York City, after Bishop Dubois' sad funeral, he proceeded to put the house of the New York Church in order. Under the old system by which church property was held in the name of lay trustees there had been many financial abuses. There had also been serious conflicts between congregations and the episcopal authority because of this trustee system. It was a situation that affected the dignity of the Church. This, Bishop Hughes, both sensitive and proud, decided he could no longer tolerate.

Of the eight churches in New York City, all of them, he found on close examination of their finances, were debt-ridden. Five were perilously close to bankruptcy. It took time, and the opposition to him was often fiery, but by a series of drastic moves he finally succeeded in abolishing the whole system of lay trustee control. He went on to consolidate the debts of the eight churches. He took title to their property in his own name and began the giant task of paying off their mortgages and seeing that they remained solvent.

The new system of church property control was ratified at the first New York Diocesan Synod held in 1842. But the months of battling with rebellious trustees had left the

Bishop ill and tired. He knew so well what it was to be thrust into a position of episcopal authority without adequate preparation. If it were the will of God many more years might extend before him. In the meantime, he felt he needed an assistant whom he could train to follow him. In May, 1843, he petitioned the Holy See for an aide.

His doctors advised that rest and a sea voyage might restore him to health; after all he was only forty-six. The Bishop finally consented to join a party that included Bishop John Purcell of Cincinnati; Father Pierre Jean De Smet, the Jesuit missionary to the Indians of the Pacific Northwest; and the powerful Republican editor and political leader, Thurlow

Bishop Hughes traveled in springless buggies on primitive roads when making parish visitations.

Weed. In Dublin, Bishop Hughes renewed his friendship with Daniel O'Connell.

After the Dublin stay the party moved on to England, landing at Liverpool. At sailing time in New York one of his friends had given Bishop Hughes two small bottles of snuff. It was one of the remedies of the day for curing or easing seasickness. Bishop Hughes had half forgotten that the two small bottles were in his traveling bag. He did not customarily take snuff and the Dublin excise men had just waved him on.

The customs officer at Liverpool looked suspiciously at the three Papist clergymen. He put a high duty of four dollars on Bishop Hughes' two small flasks of powdered tobacco. John Hughes made mild but righteous protest.

Overconscious of his uniform as an officer of Her Majesty Queen Victorias Customs, the man drew himself up in pompous dignity and proceeded to lecture Bishop Hughes.

"You must pay this, sir, for the honor of the Queen."

John Hughes took a side glance at Thurlow Weed. His eyelid drooped. Blandly he answered the little man:

"If it is for her honor then I must if I must. But what I would like to do is to give Her Majesty a good *pinch*." And in an aside to Mr. Weed he added, "Of course, I mean of this snuff." Gentle Father De Smet giggled and the customs officer glared.

In the back of his mind Bishop Hughes had consented to the trip as a working vacation rather than as a free holiday. He had hoped that in Belgium he might raise more money for his diocese. He was disappointed in this, but he did get the promise of mission priests to work among his scattered flock.

The trip abroad restored him to all his old energy. It was well it had, for there were trying times ahead for American Catholics in the year 1844. The year started well. Bishop

Hughes gave a series of lectures on Catholic doctrines each Thursday night during February that packed the cathedral, with many interested non-Catholics present. And he received the assistance he so needed when on March 10, 1844, Father John McCloskey, born in Brooklyn, was named his coadjutor bishop. Later to become the first American Cardinal, Bishop McCloskey had been also the first native New Yorker to become a secular priest.

But that year saw also the rise of a so-called Native American political party. It was bitterly anti-Catholic and its leaders, playing on prejudice, incited their followers to acts of violence against Catholic institutions. In terrifying rioting in Philadelphia, City of Brotherly Love, two churches and rectories and two convents were burned. Forty lives were sacrificed to the mobs, more than sixty people were seriously injured, and eighty-one dwelling houses were looted or destroyed.

Bishop Kenrick of Philadelphia counseled his people to bear with the outrages in the spirit of the early Christian martyrs, to return good for evil. He pleaded with them to trust to the municipal authorities and to respectable public opinion to bring the lawlessness to a halt. He refused to give his permission to Catholics to set armed guards around their churches. "Rather let every church burn than shed one drop of blood or imperil one precious soul," he said.

Much as he revered and loved his old Bishop, John Hughes had no patience with such meekness. He forthrightly issued a public statement: "If a single Catholic church is burned in New York the city will become a second Moscow."

The burning of the Russian city by Napoleon's soldiers was still vivid in people's minds as a frightful holocaust. Bishop Hughes did not need to elaborate on his words. And he took the defensive steps that Bishop Kenrick could not bring himself to take.

At the close of the election polls in April, 1844, a rabble army of some twelve hundred Nativists paraded through New York's Sixth and Fourteenth Wards, shouting insults at the Irish Catholic residents. The Philadelphia riots had their start in just such a way. Bishop Hughes had counseled restraint against all but actual physical attack. The Catholic citizens shuttered their windows and remained indoors.

The disorderly mob turned into the Bowery and swung into Spring Street heading toward their objective, St. Patrick's Cathedral on Mott Street.

"But there they halted," said John Hughes later, adding drily, "for a reason they had."

The reason was the well-armed massing about the church of two thousand members of the Ancient Order of Hibernians whose earlier establishment as a fraternal organization the Bishop had encouraged. He had not told *all* the Irish Catholics to stay within doors.

A few weeks later he acted as forcibly when a Nativist mass meeting was planned for City Hall Park and he learned that it was to be addressed by the leaders of the Philadelphia rioters. John Hughes knew that if the meeting were held the city might expect more mob violence and church burnings. He organized forces of one to two thousand men to guard every Catholic church in New York. Then he took up his blackthorn stick and marched on City Hall.

Mayor Robert H. Morris wrung his hands helplessly and asked what he should do.

"I did not come to tell you what to do. I am a churchman, not the Mayor of New York. But if I were the Mayor I would examine the laws of the state and see if there were not attached to the police force a battery of artillery and a company or so of artillery, and a squadron of horse. I think I should find that there were; and if so—*I should call them out!*"

The mass meeting was canceled. New York City was spared the shame of Philadelphia. John Hughes could be gentle; but he was "fierce when provoked," as Mayor Morris hurried to tell the incoming Nativist Mayor Harper.

4

THE SCHOOLHOUSE FIRST

Let the little children come to me

—MARK 10:14

Few men have ever tried harder than John Hughes as a boy and youth to obtain an education. He had bent his back in the fields and grubbed with his hands in the soil. It had been harder for him than for other men of his time because it was a Catholic education he wanted. In Ireland that had been outlawed. Only rarely did a wandering schoolmaster come by to form hedgerow classes hidden from the authorities.

In this New World he had grown to love so deeply, things were not much better. The few schools for the instruction of young children were poor and crowded. In New York the city's schools were operated by a private corporation, the Public School Society. This group, which distributed the funds provided by the city, was Protestant in its sympathies and the tone of the instruction under its direction.

From his first coming to New York, Bishop Hughes had urged his priests to start schools for the children under their care. Hundreds of Catholic boys and girls were growing up with little more knowledge of their Faith than the simple prayers they were taught at home and what they gleaned from the Gospels read aloud at Sunday Mass.

"The time has almost come," John Hughes said to his priests, "when we shall have to build the schoolhouse first and the church afterward." In this, as in so many things, he was more than a hundred years ahead of his time.

But because of the debts on the churches and their low income from a laboring people, the early Catholic schools were often makeshift affairs. Classes were taught in damp church basements by harried priests when they could snatch time from their other duties, or by poorly prepared laymen when they could be pressed into service. Yet the Catholic people preferred them to those operated by the Public School Society. In 1840 the Catholic schools, wretched as they were, were crowded over their limits with some five thousand children. There were another estimated five thousand Catholic children of school age who could not be taken care of.

Bishop Hughes determined to seek a portion of the municipal funds for his Catholic schools. It was his belief that, since the city's schools were privately run, his people, as equal citizens, were equally entitled to a share of the moneys they had paid in taxes. He was even willing to agree to place the parish schools under the supervision of the Public School Society in return for like assistance from the city. He felt he was being very fair.

He personally argued the Catholic school case before the Common Council but was turned down. Undaunted, he carried the case to the New York State Assembly. Although he had the support of his powerful friend, Thurlow Weed, and of Governor William H. Seward, the legislators as a whole were against him.

It was after this rebuff that John Hughes made his single venture into personal politics. Four days before the fall elections of 1841 he called a meeting of the Catholic men of the city in Carroll Hall. He presented them with a political slate of his own devising. On it were the names of men of both political parties who were friendly to him and of a few Catholics. The inclusion of the latter was an innovation. Catholics had not usually been put forward as officeholders.

On election day, Bishop Hughes' slate polled only 2,200 votes; but they were sufficient to show what could be done in more time than four days and greater organization than a single presentation by John Hughes. A shaken bunch of legislators in 1842 passed a bill placing the New York public schools under government control; the Public School Society would no longer run them. So much had John Hughes won. But the bill also forbade payment of school funds to any private or church schools. By so much he lost.

He never even dabbled in the slightest way in politics again. He defended his election slate by saying that he had only been speaking for the children under his care who could not speak for themselves. He pointed out that the greater number of the candidates he had named and endorsed were Protestant, so he could not be accused of setting one creed against another politically.

"Wise or unwise, I did what I did in what I conceived to be my duty to follow in the steps of my Master. 'Let the little children come to me,' Christ said, 'and do not hinder them, for of such is the kingdom of God.'"

In later years, however, he felt that his rash entrance into politics had been unseemly and improper. Because balloting was open then and a man's vote at once known, he made it his rule never to vote lest it might seem he was trying to influence his people in his choice of candidates. It is the only instance in which he did not stand up for his own full rights as an American citizen.

He carried that American citizenship as proudly as he wore his Bishop's purple. "I am a citizen," he once forcefully told New York's Mayor Harper. "I understand the rights of a citizen, and the duties also. I understand the genius, and Constitution and history of the country. My feelings and habits and thoughts have been so much identified with all that is American that I have almost forgotten that I was once what *you* call a 'foreigner.' "

He did cast one single vote in his life; that was in the Presidential election of 1832. As a young priest he had cast his ballot very openly for the Whig candidate, Henry Clay. But that ballot was cast in spirited defiance of a group of Philadelphia politicians who had threatened him with bodily harm if he did not encourage his people to support the other Democratic ticket. It was not wise to threaten stubborn John Hughes, whose mother used fondly to call him "Johnnie Contrary" as a boy.

Like St. Paul, Bishop Hughes felt himself a citizen of no mean city. He set himself to enrich that city by using every means in his power to raise the educational standards of those he served. The greater part of his flock was poor and unlettered. Until there could be a rise in their education and general living and working conditions, he must be their champion rather than their mild and gentle shepherd.

"The circumstances by which I have been surrounded and the character of the country and the people with whom I have to deal do not allow me to use, at all times, that meek and apostolic spirit which is so appropriate and beautiful," he commented.

Bishop Hughes was anxious to strengthen Catholic education in New York on all levels. In 1841 he had persuaded the Ladies of the Sacred Heart to come from France to found a "Select Female Academy." It was established at the corner of Houston and Mulberry streets. Its first superior was Madame Elizabeth Gallitzin, cousin of Prince Demetrius Gallitzin, "priest apostle of the Alleghenies." In March, 1842, Bishop Hughes dedicated the chapel at the academy to Our Lady of Seven Dolors. The Houston Street building soon outgrew its facilities as an academy and the Ladies of the Sacred Heart were forced to find larger quarters outside the city limits in Astoria, Long Island.

On his visits to Dublin, Bishop Hughes had been keenly interested in the work among children and young girls that Mother Catherine McCauley's Sisters of Mercy had undertaken. On his last visit he called at the convent on Baggot Street and asked if it were possible that Sisters could be missioned to him. He stressed his worry about the young girls beginning to come from Ireland to seek work and who had few respectable places to live unless they had relatives in the city.

His pleas were finally heard. In 1846 Mother Agnes O'Connor brought seven Sisters of Mercy to New York from the London convent. They established themselves on West Washington Place, dedicating their convent to St. Catherine of Siena. Within a few months they had their first postulant. She was Kitty, the youngest daughter of Mother Elizabeth Seton.

The Sisters of Mercy, too, soon outgrew their first dwelling and established their own Academy of Our Lady of Mercy in the Houston Street building earlier vacated by the Ladies of the Sacred Heart. Shortly afterward, at Bishop Hughes' request, they erected a building on adjoining land for the reception and protection of Irish emigrant girls. In the first year there were as many as 200 girls lodged at one time and 1,217 approved jobs found for these newcomers to the country.

On his Dublin visits, John Hughes had tried to obtain teachers for his boys from the Christian Brothers of Ireland but was unsuccessful. In France he had better fortune with the superiors of the Brothers of the Christian Schools. In 1849, the teaching sons of St. John Baptist de la Salle humbly started in the downtown city, the Holy Name Academy for boys that was to reach its present greatness in Manhattan College. A few years earlier, John Hughes had invited the Jesuits to take over St. John's College at Rose Hill. Insomuch, as a man of vision beyond his time, he was the founding father of Manhattan College and Fordham University.

Mother Seton's own Sisters of Charity of St. Joseph had been established in New York City as early as 1817. At the request of the Dominican Bishop John Connelly, they had come from Emmitsburg to take charge of the orphan asylum and school at St. Patrick's Cathedral. Orphans were one of John Hughes' greatest concerns and he soon saw the urgent necessity of opening a new boys' orphanage. However, when he asked Emmitsburg for a large number of Sisters to staff this institution, he received the reply that his request could not be granted; moreover, the Sisters' rule, as it now stood, no longer permitted them to take charge of male orphans.

Bishop Hughes therefore asked that the New York nuns form a separate community under his jurisdiction. The members who did not wish to remain under the new order of things were to be free to return to their motherhouse at Emmitsburg. Of the fifty Sisters in the diocese, thirty-one joined the new society called "The Sisters of Charity of St. Vincent de Paul." It is they who have kept over the years the habit and the widow's cap of Mother Seton. The others, returning to Emmitsburg, joined in affiliating the original community to the Paris congregation founded by St. Louise de Marillac whose members wear the blue habit and the flaring white cornette.

In 1845 when war with Mexico seemed close, Secretary of State James Buchanan, at President James Polk's suggestion, asked Bishop Hughes if he would go to Mexico as an unofficial envoy of the United States. Polk hoped that the rival claims of the two countries to California and Texas could be settled without bloodshed.

John Hughes consulted with his fellow bishops. They felt that dignity and propriety both for himself and his mission required that he be given official rank as an ambassador.

The matter was still being discussed when Mexican troops crossed into what the United States claimed was Texas territory. It was too late now for arbitration. The scheme to send John Hughes with an olive branch was abandoned, but it had brought him high into the nation's councils.

One instance of this was the appointment by President Polk of two Jesuits as chaplains during the Mexican War. They were the first Catholic priests to serve with the armed forces of the United States. Their appointment came at John Hughes' urging to the President. The nation's standing army at the outset of the war in 1845 numbered 7,194 soldiers, and of that number the Register of Enlistments recorded 2,135 natives of Ireland as recruits or re-enlistments. The *Freemans Journal,* the newspaper which spoke for the New York diocese, in a burst of patriotism reflecting that of Bishop Hughes, stated:

"It must be a source of pride to the Irish Catholic citizens to know that General [Zachary] Taylor's army consists of more than one half of their countrymen."

A total of 3,676 Irish-born enlisted during the two years of the war. Many of them were from New York City; but whether they were or not, they were Bishop Hughes' spiritual sons and in time of bodily danger he wanted them to have the consolations of their Faith. Today as a result of his prodding his friend, President Polk, we have the United States Military Ordinariate, with John Hughes' respective successors as military vicars and two assisting bishops as military delegates directing hundreds of Catholic chaplains.

More and more, John Hughes was being recognized by the ruling statesmen of the nation as the leading voice of the Catholics of the United States. Among his own people his name was being linked with that of Archbishop John Carroll. There had been long sad years after the death of that close friend of the founders of the nation when hate had risen against Catholics, years when their contribution to the establishment of the United States had seemed forgotten.

John Hughes pooh-poohed all talk that he had elevated Catholicism to new national recognition in his own respect.

"It is not John Joseph Hughes the man or the priest that notice is being taken of. John Carroll, yes; John Hughes, no. He was an aristocratic gentleman, well-connected, that his friends, Washington and Franklin and the rest, were proud to honor as one of themselves.

"I am only a farmer's son and a poor farm boy in my own American right. It is only that I am Bishop of New York and New York enjoys a certain kind of predominancy in the minds of Catholics; and so other Americans follow suit."

But it was soon shown that national recognition was of himself as priest and man. In 1847 national leaders such as ex-President John Quincy Adams, Stephen A. Douglas and John C. Calhoun, from different parts of the country and of opposite political beliefs, joined in inviting John Hughes to lecture before a joint session of the Congress.

The honor was signal and extraordinary, for John Hughes was bishop of a Church that only a few short years before had known the vicious and violent attacks of the American Nativists. Churches and convents in Philadelphia were only slowly arising from the ashes of their burning.

Senators and Representatives crowded the House chamber, the visitors' galleries were packed, as Bishop John Hughes ascended the speaker's rostrum. The topic he had chosen for his lecture was as near a sermon as the circumstances would diplomatically permit. "Christianity [is] the only source of moral, social, and political regeneration."

He spoke with eloquence and at times his words had the wings of a soaring eagle. But his thoughts were carefully marshaled, with one clear, logical premise following another.

Leaning forward the better to hear him was a freshman Representative to the Congress from Illinois, a long, gaunt, intent man. He had opposed the war with Mexico. Now as he fixed his great sad eyes on the speaker he wished with all his heart that this man's influence had been used to help avert it, as President Polk had wished. The principles this Catholic bishop was enunciating so clearly were not new to

Abraham Lincoln sat quietly, pondering the Bishop's words.

him. His first teacher, Master Zachariah Riney, had been a devout Irish Catholic, too—a good man of nobility of heart. He remembered having heard that Master Riney had later become a monk, a priest like this man. So deeply impressed was he that the tumult of applause that greeted the close of Bishop Hughes' speech disturbed him. He sat quiet in his seat, still pondering the speaker's words.

Abraham Lincoln said to himself thoughtfully, as cheers went up all about him: I shall never forget this occasion and I shall always remember this man whose heart speaks to mine.

A popular magazine writer, Mrs. Maury, an Englishwoman and a devout Anglican, wrote of John Hughes in 1847: "None ever regarded him with indifference. By some he is hated, by some feared, and by many loved; but his name is never pronounced unattended by some striking and expressive epithet."

She went on to say, after a series of interviews on which her article was based, that "although separated from him by my Country, my religion, and my sex," his gentlemanly charm of manner had quite vanquished her. "Serene, apart, and passionless," she described him, "and high and pure and holy. I cannot mingle him with things material. . . . Deeply conscious of his mission, he clothes religion with majesty and beauty."

Dr. Thomas Addis Emmet, grandnephew of Robert Emmet, the Irish patriot, was so impressed on meeting John Hughes that he called him "one of the most learned, tactful and polished gentlemen of his day." On the other hand, Philip Hone, a one-year Mayor of New York City in his gossipy and often malicious *Diary* wrote in 1843 that Bishop Hughes "deserved a cardinal's hat at least for what he has done in placing Irish Catholics upon the necks of native New Yorkers." Hone was a Nativist, and "Dagger John" was the name that the church-burning Nativists had applied to the man who defied them in New York.

Cardinal Gibbons was later to describe him as "active, bold, vigorous, and aggressive . . . another Joshua fighting in the valley." Yet on the other hand, Father Augustus Thebaud, who in his term as president of St. John's College, Fordham, came to know him well, admired him most for what he termed his "prudence." He acknowledged that John Hughes belonged most clearly to the Church militant, but he found his aggressiveness controlled always by his prudence. The Bishop did not get along too well with the Jesuits at times. Yet Father Thebaud wrote:

"I saw no change in him ever, either in his house at the old Cathedral or visiting the cottage of his sister, Mrs. Rodrigues, at Fordham. He was always the affectionate and pleasant companion ever ready to enjoy a laugh or to tell a story or anecdote."

Archbishop John Hughes' own estimate of himself was that he was a calm and patient man.

"I am not a man of strife and contention. My disposition is, I trust, both pacific and benevolent. As a proof of this I may mention that I have never had a personal altercation with a human being in my life—that I have never had occasion to call others, or be called myself, before any civil tribunal on the earth.

"It is true that public duty has not unfrequently forced on me the necessity of taking my stand in moral opposition to principles which I deemed injurious and unjust. But even then I trust I have made the distinction which Christian feeling suggests between the cause and the person of the advocate arrayed against me. And though I have sometimes, perhaps, been severe on my opponents I trust that it proceeded not from any malice in the heart: it came on me rather as a species of intellectual indignation at witnessing bad logic employed to defend worse bigotry."

In 1848 red-shirted Italian revolutionaries became angered with Pope Pius IX who would not actively take the part of Sardinian nationalists against Austria. The Red Shirts marched on, and seized the city of Rome. Pope Pius fled into exile, and for a brief period Giuseppe Mazzini headed a Roman republic.

As soon as news of the Pope's enforced flight reached New York, Archbishop Hughes ordered a special collection of "Peter's pence" taken up for him in all the city's churches. The people, poor as they were, responded loyally. Seven thousand dollars was gathered.

One of the Irish-American newspapers of the day suggested that the money be sent the exiled Pope secretly, "so as not to offend United States republican feeling." John Hughes snorted at the very idea. He had nothing to conceal about a free gift to a harassed servant of God.

"The American people are wise, sensible and just," he said. "And they despise the man who does not appreciate the first principles of the country in which he lives."

John Hughes wholeheartedly approved of the separation of Church and State in a republic where all citizens stood equal under God. He found no conflict in his spiritual allegiance to the Holy See and his duties, his rights and his privileges as an American citizen. He was a strong defender of the temporal power of the Pope; but even that stemmed in part from his vigorous Americanism. He felt that the Holy Father needed to have a domain of his own free of control or pressure from any political power.

5

AMERICAN AND IRISH

All praise to Saint Patrick

—TRADITIONAL HYMN

The Catholic Church and the United States of America were John Hughes two great loves. For Ireland, the land of his birth, he had a sentimental affection but it stood far below his love for America. He wanted the Irish-born under his care to look forward not backward. He was outspokenly zealous that they now consider themselves not Irishmen but Americans.

Archbishop Hughes had a great reverence for John England, the first Bishop of Charleston, South Carolina. Irish born like himself, Bishop England, a gentler man, was really more Irish-minded. But John Hughes treasured and often quoted a statement on Americanism made by the older Bishop to the Catholics of Charleston in 1831. He had read it over so often he knew it by heart, and so did many of his priests from hearing it from him.

He would glare fiercely as he repeated the first words, for he wanted them taken as a statement of his own stand: "I am no renegade to Ireland; but *I am now an American. . .*"

The Bishop would let that sink in, then he would continue to quote from Bishop England more calmly: " 'When upon your approach to the polls any person addresses you as an Irishman or a Frenchman or an Italian, or by any appellation but Carolinian or American, his language is distraint and offensive. He is either ignorant or supposes you to be so, or has some other sinister view. There is a *bribery of the affections!* There is a bribery in reminding you of the bravery and the patriotism and the generosity of the Irish. And all this is the more insulting as the object of the adulation, or the familiarity, is too plain to be mistaken. I warn you of your solemn serious obligation, that in giving your vote you recollect that you are an American!' "

To those who might murmur about the faith of the Irish people, Bishop Hughes had a firm answer. The United States was the better land in which to profess that Catholic Faith.

"In the annals of Church history there has never been a country which, in its civil and social relations, has exhibited so fair an opportunity for developing the practical harmonies of the Catholic Faith and Catholic charity as the United States."

He had no sympathy with congregations who wanted so-called national churches where nonliturgical services and sermons were given in French, German, or Italian. He knew a few words of Gaelic from his youth but he had all but dismissed them from his mind. Since English was the language of the United States he wanted his Irish sons and daughters to use it; and the same thing went without saying for those in his flock from other lands. "There is no geography for the Catholic *as* a Catholic," he announced firmly.

John Hughes even went so far, late in his life, to grumble to his friend, Secretary of State William Seward, about the Sixty-ninth, Eighty-eighth and Sixty-third New York Regiments being called "the Irish Brigade." He said: "The use of such a name is not indicative of good. It will promote rivalries and dissension. Are we also to have Scottish and German and Garibaldi brigades?"

It was not that he did not love Ireland but that he loved the United States more. He had no thought when the project of building a new cathedral was in his mind that it should be dedicated to any other than St. Patrick as the first cathedral on Mott Street had been. Even although he knew there would be confusion for a time about the two churches, he held fast to the tribute to the patron of most of his people.

He loved to talk in company on the good qualities the Irish were popularly supposed to have. His hearers might smile inwardly, if they were close to him, for they knew John Hughes was trying to describe himself as he would like to be thought of.

"Intellect, sentiment, fancy, wit, eloquence, music and poetry are, I might say," the Bishop would grow eloquent himself, "the natural and hereditary attributes of the Irish mind and the Irish heart. Don't you agree now, Fathers?"

"Would you say they were counteracted sometimes by hot temper and stubbornness, Your Lordship?" an old priest once asked slyly.

"Not at all, not at all," John Hughes answered with a trace of the hot temper—and the stubbornness—they all knew so well. Then because he was no man's fool and did have his share of Irish wit, "Of course an exception—like myself—only goes to prove the rule," he said blandly.

He always visited Ireland on his trips abroad and he was always greatly honored there. Some of his most notable addresses were made before vast audiences in Dublin and in Cork. One of the most signal honors came late in his life when he was asked to preach the sermon at the laying of the cornerstone in 1861 of the Catholic University in Dublin. A great gathering of 100,000 people cheered him, most unusually, after his eloquent sermon.

John Hughes was not by temperament any great admirer of men. Too many, especially in public life, fell short of his standards, which were rigorous. Abraham Lincoln was one of the very few to whom he gave unstinted admiration, although he warmly liked, and was liked in return, by Presidents Polk and Buchanan. But from his earliest life he had what amounted to hero worship for the Irish statesman, Daniel O'Connell. One of his public statements about the Liberator is important:

"Daniel O'Connell was not a bigot in religion—he was a liberal Catholic. Do not misunderstand me—my idea of a liberal Catholic is one who is sincere and faithful in the profession of his Faith, but who recognizes in every other human being the same right that he claims for himself; but in modem times a liberal Catholic has come to be understood as a man who makes no distinction between one creed and another. O'Connell was none of these; he believed in his religion . . . and to the close of his life he combined the dedication of a practical Catholic in his private moral life with the highest duties of a politician and a statesman . . ."

In 1846, 1847, and 1848 a plant disease rotted the potato crop throughout Ireland. Potatoes then formed the main food of the greater part of the people as rice does the poor of China. Thousands of the Irish people died, literally, of starvation. Thousands of others, their subsistence and very food destroyed, fled if they could to the United States and Canada. It was a time in Irish history known as "the Famine." But it was not really a famine. Other crops that the Irish field workers farmed for the landlords flourished. American relief ships laden with food passed other vessels carrying wheat and oats and barley, beef, pork and bacon to England for sale. That is why the term "the Great Starvation" is now often used.

John Hughes, a farmer's son, thought of it that way. He knew that if the other crops and produce that green Ireland gave forth in such abundance had been shared there would have been no famine nor the death-dealing pestilence that spread among the starving people.

"They call it God's famine!" he cried out. "No!— No! God's famine is known by the general scarcity of food which is its consequence. There is no general scarcity. But political economy, finding Ireland too poor to buy the produce of its own labor, exported that harvest to a better market and left the people to die of famine or live by alms."

Bishop Hughes' heart had long been set on building a new seminary at Rose Hill. The greatest need of the Church in the United States, he felt, was native-born priests who knew the ways and the needs of the people they were to serve. He had made arrangements for a special collection to be taken up in all the churches of the diocese for the seminary fund.

But as soon as ships began arriving in New York harbor with ever-increasing stories of famine horror, with men, women and little children dying of starvation on the Irish roadsides, Bishop Hughes canceled the seminary collection. He pleaded with his people to give even more generously than they had planned . . . but for the starving in Ireland.

"It is far, far better that our seminaries should be suspended than that so large a portion of our fellow beings be exposed to starvation."

To his secretary as he issued the new plea he said, "A seminary building is only brick and stone. These are God's people, suffering from lack of food and clothing, racked with the fever that attacks the weak. Worse fever no doubt than the cholera, and I knew the effects of that in Philadelphia. I cannot bear it! I cannot think of it patiently! Send out the letter to the pastors. But then leave me alone to collect myself. But for the will of God, John Hughes might be dying of hunger in an Irish ditch today."

Soon reports came to him that many of the Irish who had scraped up enough money for passage on what were called "coffin ships" were being victimized on their landing at New York. In his bitterness against the economic system that forced these new Irish from their country, John Hughes coined his own name for them. He called them "the crowded-outs."

It had long been the custom in Ireland, as in other countries when emigration seemed the only way to a better life, to send out the oldest or strongest first. Once established they would send for others in a family. It had been so in John Hughes' own case. First the father and elder brother, then John in turn, then the mother and sisters. In the days when immigration into the United States was low, the only real danger was in a stormy passage. But now things had changed.

The flood of immigrants in the famine years were fairly

safe in the crowded coffin ships. It was ashore that evil waited them. They were set upon by thugs and thieves. Unless they had relatives to meet them they were steered by "runners" to disreputable boardinghouses where they were robbed or swindled of the little money they had. The plight of lone Irish girls in a strange land was a special horror.

It was to protect these girls, hopefully and prayerfully sent out from Cork or Kerry, that the moneys they earned might help their families, that Bishop Hughes had encouraged the Sisters of Mercy to build their Houston Street refuge. He had also in 1841 given his approving blessing to the merchant, Robert Hogan, in founding the Irish Emigrant Society. Dr. William J. MacNeven, the Irish patriot of the 1798 rebellion, became the first president.

The society grew from small beginnings. When the famine immigration flood came, it was in a sturdy position to give help to the friendless, meeting incoming ships and protecting and finding work for the bewildered newcomers. Bishop Hughes used its good offices freely for sending moneys to Ireland. He had announced that he would serve as a transmitting agent for individual contributions to Ireland from friends and relatives in any amount over an English pound.

Under the urging of the Bishop, the officials of the Emigrant Society in 1847 petitioned the New York Legislature to take action to protect the health and interests of the immigrants crowding the port of New York. John Hughes further enlisted the powerful aid of his good friend, Thurlow Weed, and the political skill of another friend, Andrew Carrigan, a produce merchant and treasurer of the Catholic Orphan Asylum. As a result came the creation of the New York Commission of Emigration. Emigrants ill with contagious diseases were hospitalized and quarantined.

Refuge was established for those in need and the aged and for waifs and orphans.

Gregory Dillon, president of the Irish Emigrant Society, reported regularly to Bishop Hughes on his supervision, without pay, of the services provided under the name of the Commissioners of Immigration. It was as a result of Bishop Hughes' confidence in the Emigrant Society in handling the funds he entrusted them with, and with his encouragement, that the same group established the Emigrant Industrial Savings Bank in 1850.

Bishop Hughes had little use for those leaders of the Young Ireland movement who fled to New York after the failure of the Irish Rising of 1848. Their personalities grated upon him. Furthermore, in his strict Americanism, he thought they should keep their plotting for a free Ireland at home and not use the United States as a revolutionary base. Like his hero, Daniel O'Connell, he abhorred physical force as a means to free Ireland.

However, Bishop Hughes' heart had been so torn by the horror of the years of the Great Starvation that when news reached New York of the start of the 1848 rebellion he gave the rising his endorsement. After a great debate with himself he accompanied Horace Greeley to a great mass meeting at Vauxhall Garden in support of the new Irish rebellions.

He was so stirred by the enthusiasm of the cheering crowds at the meeting—and perhaps by memories of the bayonets that had been pressed against his own breast when he was a boy—that he rose to speak when his name was insistently shouted. He had not intended to do other than sit on the platform.

The crowd went wild with excitement when he announced that he was giving $500 to the Irish cause. He motioned them to quiet, and said, "I come to you not as a bishop and not as an Irishman but as a citizen of a country dedicated to freedom. I offer my contribution, too, not as a sword but as a shield for the innocent who may be in for a time of suffering. And I say this to you, if the men of Ireland of this day are as worthy of their fatherland as their forebears, they will do two things. One, is that in battle they will be as brave as their nation. The other is that after the battle is over they will be as humane."

The rebellion was soon put down. Bishop Hughes then promptly asked the New York committee that his donation of $500 be given to the Sisters of Mercy for their work with immigrant girls. He did not like to see his good money wasted. He felt himself taken in. When he had gone so far as to give his blessing to the rebellion, no doubt he thought his side should have won.

That may have had something to do with his distrust of and antagonism toward three of the most famous leaders of the 1848 rebellion who found refuge in New York: Thomas D'Arcy McGee, John Mitchel, and Thomas Francis Meagher. Both Mitchel and Meagher escaped to America from a penal colony in Australia and were greeted as heroes by everyone except John Hughes.

The seizure of Rome and the enforced exile of Pope Pius had soured John Hughes on all revolutionary movements. When Louis Kossuth, the leader of the Hungarian uprising, came to New York and was wildly greeted as a patriot, Bishop Hughes was outspoken against him. In his controversies with McGee, Meagher, and Mitchel, the language on both sides became very extreme by present-day standards.

John Hughes expressed his annoyance forcibly. "There

is no people in the world, whether at home or abroad, so overdosed with counsel and advice as the Irish. Their friends advise them, their enemies advise them and those who are indifferent about their welfare advise them in like manner." John Hughes was hurt that in some instances they were turning from his advice as their shepherd. He pleaded his case publicly that he might not be misunderstood.

"The Catholic Church is not a party to the politics of any nation, at home or abroad. Her mission is to all nations and to all parties in each, except as either may be divided from the other by the eternal principles of right and wrong. She can never give up her message and mission to all for the sake of some."

But John Hughes' main concern at all times was that the transplanted Irish under his charge should keep fast the Faith of their fathers. It was that concern for their souls that set John Hughes firmly against any proposed schemes for mass settlement of the thronging Irish immigrants on farmlands in the West. Early as a bishop he had discussed such plans with Thurlow Weed and Governor William Seward. They had convinced him that Irish colonies in the opening West were impracticable. One of the things that weighed most heavily with John Hughes was the shortage of priests in the country. A pioneer Irish settlement that was not builded on God and that did not have a church as its center was unthinkable. And priests were simply not available to accompany and guide and guard the faith and morals of new settlers in the Western wilderness. Bishop Hughes had not enough priests by half for his own diocesan needs.

An Irish Emigrant Aid Convention to discuss plans for such colonization, held in Buffalo in 1856, drew his great disapproval. It was a Catholic convention, opening with solemn Mass in the Buffalo Cathedral, and with clergy from the United States and Canada in attendance. A number of Western bishops gave financial support to the convention's plan to buy Western land for colonies. John Hughes roundly denounced the whole scheme and by his influence brought it to naught.

Later exponents of directed settling of Catholics in the West like Archbishop John Ireland of St. Paul and Bishop John Lancaster Spalding deplored what they thought was John Hughes' shortsightedness. Ten years later Archbishop Hughes had somewhat modified his own views; but the overwhelming masses of the Irish, for better or worse, were fixed in the Eastern cities then. The farming talents they might have brought to the West were rusted from disuse. Only a few valiant families, comparatively speaking, rode in the covered wagons behind the oxen for the building of the Western nation.

Despite his firm insistence that he was an American and *only* an American, John Hughes treasured his Irish blood. He could talk sentimentally of a link of speech that drew him closer in friendship to Marshal Nugent, head of the Austrian Army, whom he had met in Vienna on his begging trip to the Leopoldine Society.

"What especially endeared me to him was that he did not try to get rid of his brogue. He preserved and cherished it as a pleasing peculiarity to his speech. Ah, his delicate brogue reminded me of the gold which fringes a cloud when the sun is setting or tips the supreme point of a lightning rod."

John Hughes had no brogue of his own since that way of speaking English is a heritage from the mode of speech of the English of Elizabethan times. It is common in the south of

Ireland where it was the speech of Spenser and Raleigh. John Hughes was from Tyrone in the north where what slight accent there is is Scottish-tinged.

Only very rarely did John Hughes attend the banquets or dinners of the Friendly Sons of St. Patrick, the most distinguished Irish society since Revolutionary times and of which, in Philadelphia, George Washington was an honorary member. From the time of Hughes' bishopric he went out very little into society of any kind.

In the earlier years of New York's historic St. Patrick's Day parade, it was held in the morning and in the lower city. The parade then ended always at St. Patrick's old cathedral on Mott Street, where Bishop Hughes either presided at solemn Mass or preached the sermon.

John Hughes always was ready to affirm the great contribution his former countrymen had made to the formation and building of the United States. In 1852 he gave a notable lecture on "The Catholic Chapter in the History of the United States." He had it published and sent a copy to a friend in Philadelphia, a member of the distinguished Biddle

The parade always ended at old St. Patrick's Cathedral.

family.

To his delight, Mr. Biddle wrote back, "My late father always said that during this contest [the Revolutionary War] the rank and file of the best disciplined and most continental regiments of the Pennsylvania line were chiefly Irish Catholics; and three of these very religious regiments were commanded by the sons of Irishmen: namely Wayne, Irvine, and Shea—the former the distinguished favorite of Washington and all three afterward generals."

He went on to mention Stephen Moylan, Major Butts,

Colonel Keating, and Colonel Sharp and to say that most of the soldiers with General Wayne when he stormed Stony Point were Irish.

John Hughes treasured the letter. It proved what he had always thought—a true Irishman made the truest of Americans.

6

NEW YORK'S ARCHBISHOP

Reading maketh a full man, conference a ready man.

—FRANCIS BACON, ESSAY "OF STUDIES"

In the fall of 1850 Pope Pius IX erected the diocese of New York into an archdiocese with John Hughes as its first archbishop. A few years earlier Albany and Buffalo had been cut off from the parent diocese and given their own bishops; these sees, together with Boston and Hartford, were now placed under the jurisdiction of Archbishop Hughes.

He journeyed to Rome to receive the pallium, the band of white wool marked with black crosses that is the especial mark of his office. Pope Pius IX personally placed the pallium about his neck.

The ninth Pius, but recently returned from his exile, showed toward John Hughes the same fatherly affection as had Pope Gregory XVI. In his youth the Holy Father had served in a minor post as auditor to the apostolic delegate to

Chile. It had given him a feeling that he was well acquainted with America. He told Archbishop Hughes it was an extra bond between them and persisted in talking of New York as if it were a replica of the South American cities he had known. The Archbishop held his peace. Had it been a lesser man, even a cardinal, he would forthrightly have given him facts and figures, proud as he was of his city. The Vicar of Christ on earth he would never presume to correct.

In Rome during that stay John Hughes found himself a noteworthy figure. The beggar Bishop of an earlier day was now honored and courted. His gifts as a preacher were signally recognized and he was asked to give a series of sermons at the Church of Sant' Andrea delle Frate.

It was no secret that the United States Minister to the Vatican had hinted to Pope Pius that John Hughes was of cardinal's stature. The suggestion may have originated with President Zachary Taylor, "Old Rough and Ready," who commanded the United States Army in the Mexican War. He would have known how highly John Hughes was regarded by former Presidents Polk and Buchanan and by one of his own staunch supporters, the Archbishop's close friend Thurlow Weed.

However, the College of Cardinals was then limited to seventy and the roster at the time was filled. Pope Pius is said sincerely to have regretted that "there are no openings."

But when the possibility of the bestowal of the red hat when a vacancy came was rumored, some of the other United States Bishops made quiet objections to Rome. It was not that they begrudged John Hughes the honor. They felt that the spirit of the day in the United States made the time inopportune. The anti-Catholic "Know-Nothing" movement was growing. Some non-Catholics might associate the presence of a prince of the Church in the United States with some supposed papal plot to take over the country.

From the time of his consecration as assistant Bishop, John Hughes had lived in fairly humble quarters at 263 Mulberry Street behind old St. Patrick's Cathedral. It was a simple house, half offices, half rectory that had been rather grudgingly bought for Bishop Dubois in 1836.

Even when John Hughes became Bishop of New York in his own right, he stayed on there contentedly with his assistant clergy. He liked its closeness to his cathedral and it was not too far from the mother church of St. Peter's on Barclay Street. When the old cathedral was built there had been complaints that it was too far out from the city. The first sexton grumbled about foxes prowling in the churchyard. Now the crowded city was creeping past it.

Bishop Hughes did not mind the inadequacies of his house, little as it resembled the episcopal residences and bishops' palaces in which he had been a guest abroad. He liked being among the greater part of his people. It might be said he liked having his eagle eye upon them.

And at Mulberry and Houston streets were the convent buildings he liked to visit in a short relaxing walk. When the Ladies of the Sacred Heart had their academy there, he enjoyed talking with the French nuns about Paris, of Notre Dame Cathedral which he so admired, and of the deposed King Louis Philippe, who had been his friend.

When the Ladies of the Sacred Heart removed their select academy to Astoria, he had installed the Sisters of Mercy in the old building. There he visited them even more frequently than in their first convent on West Washington Place. He told the superior, Mother Agnes O'Connor, that in the Irish phrase it was becoming to him "a home away from home," a place where he could chat easily with nuns by the names of Horan, O'Doherty, Byrne, and Breen. If they knew he was coming, the Irish Sisters would bake him soda bread or the oaten cakes of his Tyrone childhood.

The primary work of the Mercy Sisters was to visit the sick poor. Bishop Hughes was continuously sending to the convent the names of those who had made personal appeal to him. On his next visit to the convent he would want to know all about the Sisters' visits.

Once their habit became somewhat familiar in the city, he encouraged them in another work of mercy that Mother McAuley had instituted in Dublin: the visiting of prisons. The Sisters' dress did not seem at all strange in the prison where so few kindly people came. Three times a week two Sisters visited the men and boys in The Tombs, New York City's jail. Once a month two Sisters visited Sing Sing prison. In that day, long before the time of visiting nurses or social workers, they were looked upon in both places not only as Sisters but as Angels of Mercy.

If one of his friends in the hierarchy were visiting him, Bishop John Timon of Buffalo or Bishop William Quarter, first Bishop of Chicago, sometime during their stay he would walk them over to St. Catherine's Convent and the House of Mercy. He enjoyed showing off the sewing rooms and the comfortable home they provided for the immigrant working girls.

The purpose of the Ladies of the Sacred Heart was primarily the education of girls of good family. Mother Madeline Sophie Barat had instituted the congregation to restore finer education for girls after the horrors of the French Revolution. On the whole the society preferred to operate their schools as boarding academies. The need for elementary Catholic education in New York City was so great, however, that Bishop Hughes asked Mother Hardey, with Mother Barat's consent, to open a day school on Bleecker Street at the corner of Laurens. It was in charge of Mother Sarah Jones.

When the Jesuit Fathers opened their church and college dedicated to St. Francis Xavier in 1850, the Bleecker Street nuns moved to a house at 64 West Fourteenth Street and opened a school in St. Francis' Church basement. It was another of Bishop Hughes' forward thinking plans for the Catholic education of the children in his charge.

Soon the Ladies of the Sacred Heart taught a parish school of 600 girls. They also enrolled 80 girls of wealthier parents in a day academy. Their work spread out. In this earliest period 70 working girls attended night school and there were 150 pupils in the Sunday school. So great was the enthusiasm of the people and so glowing the reports brought home by the children that the nuns were moved to start classes for older women.

"Some of them are utterly ignorant of some matters in the religion they profess, but they are so eager to learn," Mother Jones reported to Bishop Hughes.

In 1842 a villa, really a summer cottage, had been bought for the Bishop's personal use in far-out Manhattanville. At first he thought he would like it, although the house itself, like all summer places, was not suited to changes in the weather. He was happiest in it when the Ladies of the Sacred Heart bought the Lorillard estate fairly close by and moved from Astoria to establish their academy there. Once again he resumed his walks and talks with the nuns. He greatly admired the superior, Mother Aloysia Hardey who became one of his closest friends.

Mother Hardey was a wise and serene woman whom he often consulted on educational problems. He valued her counsel highly. He went to the convent almost daily when the nuns were moving in. He was much amused by the makeshift furniture they were forced to use in restarting the school. "Is this crate meant for a chair or a table?" he would say.

The boarders at the academy wore a uniform of bottle green merino. He would gently tease Mother Hardey that the color was in his honor and that even the most French of the nuns were being coaxed into being Irish.

In summer the girls wore light-colored frocks on Wednesdays and Sundays, pink and blue and white in turn.

"I am beginning to suspect, Reverend Mother," John Hughes said one day with a twinkle, "that you have a spy at the villa and switch the girls into colors to suit my own moods. Blue when I am feeling downhearted, pink when I am feeling rosy, and white when I am in a white heat over some project—as I am now."

The project was that the nuns establish a free school for the Catholic children of the neighborhood. Bishop Hughes thought that the unused brick stable on the property, with a little alteration, would make a splendid schoolhouse. Soon the Ladies were teaching 100 girls of the neighborhood and their chaplain 100 boys. Again at Bishop Hughes' wish, the nuns departed from their customs to take temporary care of 20 orphans whose parents had died in an epidemic of the dread cholera.

He delighted to preside at the yearly prize-giving exercises and to attend the school picnic on nearby grounds at the close of the spring term.

It was at his request that the nuns gave shelter at Manhattanville to Bishop Pelagio de Lebastida, who had been expelled from Mexico by an anti-clerical President. The Bishop of Puebla de Los Angeles lived at the convent for a year, confirming, presiding at professions, and acting in all ways as a gentle if august chaplain.

The Mexican President, Ignacio Cononfort, as it happened, had two daughters boarding at the school. The nuns rightly became flustered when a message came that he was in New York and planning to visit them. Mother Hardey sent in haste for Bishop Hughes who escorted Bishop de Lebastida to his own house where he entertained him until word came from the convent that the Mexican President had departed.

Later John Hughes told Mother Hardey, "Ordinarily in the case of such a distinguished guest I would have been impelled to go over and formally greet him. I had half a mind, indeed, to do so while the good Bishop was resting. It was never my way to be an Achilles sulking in his tent."

"It was just as well, dear Bishop," said Mother Hardey calmly, "the meeting might have been—awkward."

"Awkward wouldn't have been the name for it," said John Hughes, "I would have given the rascal a piece of my mind."

" 'Blessed are the meek.' " Mother Hardey's eye had a slight twinkle. John Hughes snorted, then grinned and shook hands with her.

But his Manhattanville villa never pleased John Hughes. He was not happy to be so far out of things. The trip up and down town on the Harlem Railway was long and tedious. The steamcars were uncomfortable riding, stuffy if the windows were closed; filled with smoke and cinders from the engine if they were opened. He now had a horse and carriage but to use them took even longer, and the unpaved roads out of the city were alternately dusty or muddy.

"Dislike for this house grows on me," he told Mother

Hardey. "It is cold in winter and hot in summer. Again, there is no room for a library and I have become so accustomed to being surrounded by books that I feel lonely in the evenings beyond measure."

This longing for his books is his own statement. Yet a historian of his times wrongly commented that while "In character with his countrymen he is a confirmed newspaper reader. . . . He rarely read a book." John Hughes was an avid newspaper reader in his anxiety to keep himself informed on all the issues of the day. But books were a deeper joy of his heart's desiring.

He read deeply and widely. He bought advertised books he thought might interest him and received many as gifts from the publishers of the day. When he particularly delighted in a book he autographed it and sent it to one of his many cultured friends for their enjoyment.

The Manhattanville cottage was finally sold and a properly dignified residence bought for the Archbishop at 218 Madison Avenue. It was on the northwest corner of Thirty-sixth Street, across from what is now the Morgan Library.

He brought his sister, Mrs. Rodrigues, with her husband and child from Fordham Village to manage his simple household. He had his chamber and study on the second floor. The fourth floor was given over to his library which extended the full depth of the house. It consisted of about 10,000 volumes. Most of the books were on theology, but he also possessed many rare and valuable books on other subjects that had been given to him. It was his boast that he had read them all; none of them were for show. As a young priest in Philadelphia he had been a close friend of Mathew Carey, the first great Catholic publisher and pamphleteer. Carey sent him copies of the pamphlets he wrote in his later years as soon as they were off the presses. John Hughes read them carefully and made his own comments in the margins. Later on, however, he gave up that early habit, thinking it defaced his books.

Among the treasures of his library was a large collection of original letters and documents on early American Catholic history. They came from the library of his old friend and teacher, Father Brute, who had become Bishop of Vincennes, Indiana. When Bishop Brute died, his successor, Bishop Celestine de la Hailandiere, had the historic collection sent to John Hughes who he felt would most value them. Father James Roosevelt Bayley, nephew of Mother Seton, when he was Archbishop Hughes' secretary, used them as a source for his *Brief Sketch of the History of the Catholic Church on the Island of New York.*

The library was at times a source of minor annoyance to Father Bayley and the other secretaries in turn. John Hughes lent his books freely and kept no account of the lending. Besides he had a habit of taking books down to his study, and if he took a book from the shelves to an adjacent table he never thought of returning it to its proper space.

It was his frequent complaint to Father Bayley. "It is very strange. This library is supposed to be catalogued, but I simply cannot understand how it is arranged. I can never for the life of me find anything in it."

Father Bayley would sigh inwardly and make a mental note to have the cataloguer back to recheck the shelves. All would be well for a few weeks, then the Archbishop's bookishness and absentmindedness would bring confusion again.

He was an active collector of paintings and the house was adorned with many objects of art that had been presented to him on his trips abroad. It was at the Madison Avenue

The Archbishop's library was filled with rare and valuable books.

house that he presumably sat, or stood, for the painting by George P. A. Healy, the artist of note in that day who had made portraits, among other importantly placed personages, of Abraham Lincoln and Pope Pius IX.

The Archbishop lived alone in the house save for his secretary and his sister and her family. His curates remained in the house on Mulberry Street where he kept his offices.

He was very sparing in food and drink. Eating he considered a duty, not a pleasure. He took no breakfast save a cup of coffee after Mass in his chapel. Then on most days he rode in his simple carriage to Mulberry Street. He often took no food until five or six o'clock in the evening when the day's work was done. Even when he was at home he rarely appeared for dinner which was at two o'clock.

Father Bayley for a time persuaded him to accept invitations to dinner and to entertain a little himself. But he preferred his books and his writing; soon he was back in his rather lonely evening habits. He held to only one social custom. On St. Patrick's Day he invited the clergy of the city to dine.

At one time he had a billiard table installed in the house. The game was fashionable at the time. But for him there was none of the laying of small bets and cigar-smoking rivalry of the gentlemen of fashion. He played the game alone against an imaginary opponent. Another time he began the study of astronomy and the globes and had a telescope mounted on the roof of the stable where he would spend silent night hours searching the heavens. Most often when he was lonesome and wanted conversation, he would drop into the office of his secretary, which was next to his study, and perch on a high stool and talk. His only really close lay friend in the city was a merchant, Peter Hargous.

Archbishop Hughes was not a tall man—five feet nine—

although in the pulpit especially his great dignity made him seem so. His build was rugged although his health was never strong. He had early become bald, and from the time of his consecration as Auxiliary Bishop he wore a scratch wig. That is one that only partially covers the head but is larger than a toupee. At home and at his offices he wore the purple cassock of a bishop with red buttons and a doctor's short cape. In public the only sign of his office was a purple stock. Roman collars had not come into use. Clergymen wore black in the fashion of the day and the close-fitting wide band of black about their neck that other gentlemen wore.

John Hughes lived comfortably on the $3,000—in 1857 raised to $5,000—that the archdiocese granted him for his maintenance and expenses. Save for books and an occasional painting that pleased him he spent little money on himself.

His personal indifference to money was so great that it was another vexation for his secretaries. When checkbooks came into use he frankly called them "a botheration." He could not teach himself to fill out the stubs. When he sat down to balance his checkbook account it was done with groans and sighs.

"Father Bayley, Father Bayley, it very clearly shows here as I read these tormenting figures that you owe me a certain sum of money. Do you deny it, boy?"

"Not at all, Your Grace. Not from the evidence you have in your hand. But if you will take a look at this other statement you will find that you borrowed the money from me in the first place."

"So I did, so I did. My mistake. Think nothing of it. But if it weren't from the Emigrant Bank, whose officers I know so well, I'd think they had an Orangeman mix up my account just to plague me."

When Archbishop Hughes went on a trip outside the city

his secretary would give him two paper packets of gold and silver currency. He never carried a wallet or pocketbook. No matter how short or long the journey or the amount of the coins, the Archbishop never failed to arrive home with empty pockets. What he did not use he gave freely to the needy he had encountered or to a pastor he had visited, for the parish poor. Only the fact that he disliked to carry money saved him from being at the mercy of every beggar about Mulberry Street. He could not say "No."

His relations with his priests were warm and friendly. He was never overstrict in his government of his clergy. He gave them his trust and expected that they had like trust in him. If a priest made a mistake and he had to call him in to the chancery office, his correction was fatherly. "See it doesn't happen again," was his severest reproof. But a lie, even a white lie, he could not tolerate. Unhappy the priest or layman he caught in what seemed a falsehood. He would thunder at him with all the mighty force of his voice and wrath. Then, like as not when he felt the culprit had learned his lesson, he would send him away with a smile and his blessing.

He was a keen judge of men. In time he was to be called the "Father of Bishops" because so many of the assistants he chose were raised to the episcopacy. Father Bayley became the first Bishop of Newark, New Jersey; Father Loughlin, his vicar general became first Bishop of Brooklyn; Father John McCloskey became Bishop of Albany and then his successor in New York; Father John J. Conroy succeeded Bishop McCloskey in Albany; Father David Bacon became first Bishop of Portland, Maine; Father Bernard O'Reilly and Father Francis P. MacFarland became the successive Bishops of Hartford, Connecticut; Father Andrew Byrne became the first Bishop of Little Rock, Arkansas; and Father William

G. McCloskey became the fourth Bishop of Louisville, Kentucky. They were all trained under John Hughes.

Throughout his life, he was as successful in winning converts to the Church as he had been as a priest in Philadelphia. At the end of 1849 his official register notes that four prominent New York ministers had come into the Church: John Murray Forbes, rector of St. Luke's Episcopal Church; Thomas Scott Preston, his assistant; Donald McLeod and Jedidiah Huntington. McLeod and Preston became priests. The latter, later a monsignor, was the founder of the Sisters of the Divine Compassion. Another young convert, John Rose Green Hassard, he employed for a time as his secretary. Hassard was to become the first editor of *The Catholic World* and to write an early biography of his patron.

When Levi Silliman Ives resigned as the first Protestant Episcopal Bishop of North Carolina to become a Catholic, John Hughes was much concerned over the problem of finding him suitable employment on which he could support his wife and children. The Archbishop made room for him among the professors at St. John's College, Fordham, and arranged for lectures in other Catholic schools. He used all the means at his disposal to ensure that Ives be given the respect to which his late position had entitled him.

In the 1850's a new anti-Catholic movement was sweeping over the United States. It gained more members among the bigoted and the ignorant than the earlier Nativist movement. It grew into a political party that in some states, notably Massachusetts, put its candidates into high office. It was the policy of members to say "I know nothing" if they were questioned. Hence those who belonged to the party were called "Know-Nothings."

The strong personality of John Hughes spared New York City from disorders, although there was anti- Catholic rioting in Brooklyn and in many other cities across the nation.

In 1853, Pope Pius IX appointed Archbishop Cajetan Bedini to be Apostolic Nuncio to Brazil. The Holy Father, finding that Monsignor Bedini was sailing by way of New York, asked him to make a survey of ecclesiastical matters in the United States. He gave him an autographed letter of greeting and good will to President Franklin Pierce.

Archbishop Hughes greeted Archbishop Bedini warmly and arranged for the visit to Washington where Mr. Pierce received him courteously and cordially. The Nuncio to Brazil then humbly asked if he could place himself under John Hughes' wing; America was so strange to him.

Together the two prelates journeyed in July to Milwaukee for the consecration of the cathedral there. On October 30, 1853, Archbishop Bedini presided at old St. Patrick's at the consecration of James Roosevelt Bayley as Bishop of Newark, John Loughlin as Bishop of Brooklyn and Louis de Goesbriand as Bishop of Burlington, Vermont. As consecrator, everyone remarked on the majesty and dignity with which Archbishop Bedini conducted the long services.

John Hughes' health had, in his own words, been "infirm and uncertain" during the year. Sea voyages always helped him. So when Monsignor Bedini left on a Middle Western tour, Archbishop Hughes took time off for a short holiday in Cuba.

On the ship were three Redemptorist priests who later were to found the Paulist Fathers or Congregation of St. Paul: Fathers Isaac Hecker, Augustine Hewit, and Clarence Walworth. The *Crescent* was to make its first stop at New

Orleans, and they were to preach a mission there. Father Hecker, who had served as chaplain to the Sisters of Mercy at St. Catherine's, was an especial friend. The Archbishop's tired spirits were soon revived by the sea air, rest and good talk and he returned from this trip with health much restored.

However, while Archbishop Hughes was away, Monsignor Bedini was having a most distressing time. A renegade Italian priest, Alessandro Gavazzi, who had joined forces with the Know-Nothing anti-Catholics, singled out gentle Archbishop Bedini for especial abuse. It was the old story. The Pope planned to take over the United States and had sent the Archbishop to survey the ground, and other nonsense of that sort.

In Pittsburgh, Louisville, Kentucky, and Cincinnati, Archbishop Bedini was the center of outrageous attacks, and even one attempt upon his life. He cut short his trip and returned sadly to New York to embark for Brazil. At New York, the Mayor was so afraid of disturbances that he would not allow this distinguished visitor—who had been received by the President— to leave the country properly. He insisted that he go by night to Staten Island where a small boat would put him on board his ship the *Atlantic* which had orders to put by for him.

This shameful treatment of a man whom he admired and cherished, who had been his own house guest, was only made known to John Hughes on his return to New York. His anger was great. He wrote to Archbishop Bedini at once:

"If I had been in New York we should have taken a carriage at my door, even an open one if the day had been fine enough; and gone by the ordinary streets to the steamboat on which you were to embark. You will, perhaps, be astonished when I add that in such an event, notwithstanding the lying clamors of the telegraph wires and the newspapers, I do not believe that violence or insult would be offered to you or to me or to any of our party." The eagle of American Catholics, with eyes and beak and wings and claw would, in such instance, have frightened the boldest ruffian in the carriage's path.

It especially hurt John Hughes to find a gentle note from Monsignor Bedini thanking him for his many courtesies, and a farewell gift of a fine clock. This clock became one of his dearest treasures.

John Hughes had been personally friendly with a series of United States Presidents, from James Polk on. President Millard Fillmore had entertained him privately at dinner in the White House.

When, shortly after his inauguration in 1857, President James Buchanan heard that the Archbishop of New York would pass through Washington on a trip South to deliver an address, he asked him to be his overnight guest.

Since Know-Nothingism was just beginning to die down, John Hughes thought it better to decline an invitation that might give rise to misunderstandings. But he did it in one of his most gay and friendly letters:

"Your invitation is very flattering and I should have no hesitation in accepting it, the less because Miss Lane is my great friend as well as her esteemed and honored Uncle. If you still lived at Wheatlands in Pennsylvania I would throw myself on your Bachelor hospitality with or without an invitation, knowing the generous feeling of your Irish ancestors is by no means worn out in your breast."

Miss Harriet Lane was President Buchanans official hostess. Archbishop Hughes had known her when she was a student at the Convent of the Visitation in Georgetown, where, he declared to her uncle, she was "the princess of the Academy. That I thought and- still believe."

The ever-growing signs of recognition that were given him by important men in important places John Hughes thought of in terms of his Church and his place in it as Archbishop of New York; not of himself.

"In all my life," he wrote, "I have never meddled directly or indirectly with the political affairs of this country. And yet, even among public men from the President down there are very few who are not under the impression that a spoken word of mine, or even a hint, is sufficient to vibrate especially among Catholics from one extremity of the United States to the other. I have long ceased to trouble myself about this erroneous impression."

7

"Where Thy Glory Dwelleth"

From his Madison Avenue house, on days when there was no pressure of business downtown at the chancery office, John Hughes liked to drive north into the countryside.

They were never merely pleasure drives. If he had the time and it was a fine day he might go as far up as 132nd Street and Broadway where the Christian Brothers had established their Academy of the Holy Infancy. He often urged them to expand their work in the free schools about the city in which they were teaching.

Often he would visit the Sisters of Charity at their Academy of Mount St. Vincent at McGowan's Pass at 107th Street in what is now Central Park. When the park began to encroach upon the academy grounds, he was able to obtain for the Sisters Fonthill Castle, the estate of the eminent actor Edwin Forrest at Riverdale. He handled the negotiations so smoothly that he was able to charm Mr. Forrest into making a gift of $5,000 to the Sisters outside of the terms of the sale.

Archbishop Hughes had a certain family interest in the Sisters of Charity, for, as we know, his sister Ellen had become Sister Mary Angela in the congregation. In 1849 she had established St. Vincent's Hospital in two small houses with thirty beds at Seventh Avenue and 11th Street in Greenwich Village.

Most often on a short ride he liked to visit with the orphans at the home the daughters of Mother Seton had under their care at 51st Street on the Fifth Avenue. From his earliest days he had felt it one of the especial duties of his priesthood to be father to the fatherless. Below the orphanage, stretching from the Middle Road (Fifth Avenue) eastward past Madison Avenue, was a large stretch of vacant land that in 1852 had become cathedral property. For years it had been considered of little value.

It had first come into Church hands in 1810 when the Jesuit Father Vincent Kohlmann, then vicar general of the new diocese, had paid $11,000 for a waste tract running back to Fourth Avenue. Two trustees, Andrew Morris and Cornelius Heeney, the great Catholic philanthropist of the day, took title to the land.

On the property Father Kohlmann opened the New York Literary Institute which may be said to be the forerunner of Fordham University. It was much too far from the city to be a success and soon closed its doors. The land was held in title by various Catholic trustees until 1827.

By that year graves were beginning to crowd each other in old St. Patrick's churchyard. Churchyard burial—in God's half acre—was an old and loved custom that could no longer be carried out. The land uptown on the Middle Road was a possible cemetery site. The trustees of St. Patrick's joined with those of St. Peter's and St. Mary's and had the deed to it conferred to them by Dennis Doyle who then held the title. But the cemetery plan fell through. Surveyor tests showed the land had a rock base in parts that made it not suitable as a burying ground. Now it was in John Hughes' possession. He abhorred waste; he hated to let the land lie idle; but he did not quite know what to do with it. He knew it would increase in value as the city moved northward, so he did not want to sell it too soon.

Once, whimsically, John Hughes had described himself as "a church builder by trade." The erection of new churches had been one of his greatest satisfactions. When he was a boy in Ireland there had been no church. The Catholic people could worship only secretly, high on the mountains, with Mass said on a flat rock and guards posted to warn lest the soldiery come and seize the priest who had a price on his head. Only occasionally was it safe to have Mass said in a farm kitchen. Even in Dublin, where things were a little easier, one of the churches was known as Adam and Eve's because it was hidden behind a tavern of that name.

It was one of his dreams as Archbishop of New York to build a more dignified and lovelier cathedral than that on Mott Street. He had watched with interest the building of the new Trinity Church by the Episcopalian diocese of New York. It was being spoken of as worthy of cathedral status. For himself he preferred the lines of the new Grace Church. He had made a note of the architect, James Renwick, Jr., son of a Columbia University professor. He liked his use of the ornamental Gothic. The cathedral of his own dreams would be Gothic. Renwick might be the man for him.

Father Bayley drove out with the Archbishop one day to the orphanage on Fifth Avenue. As they were leaving, one of the Sisters called the priest back for a message. When he returned to the carriage the coachman said, "His Lordship the Archbishop told me to tell you to join him. I don't know where he's got to. He took a walk over there in the brush and I kind of lost sight of him."

The brambles tore at Father Bayley's long coat as he pushed his way through the bushes and long grass. He found the Archbishop in that part of the tract nearest to the Middle Road. He was gazing eastward and seemed in a reverie, leaning on his stick, but his eyes were lifted rather than cast down in meditation. Father Bayley waited respectfully.

The Archbishop called him closer. He prodded at the ground with his stick. "Father, this is the place, in the heart of a city expanded beyond our present contemplation, where a hundred years from now our Catholic Faith will be most hallowed. This is where, please God, I shall build the new cathedral."

Half to his companion, half to himself he went on musingly: "The city is built on an island. The movement of its growth must always be northward. I see it going past my own house, creeping up on it and going past, far out as that dwelling is. I can see the city sweeping past this once outlying village of Elgin up to Yorkville and Haarlem, to Bloomingdale and Riverdale, taking to itself all the little villages. Yes, even up and beyond Morrisania and what was once old Jonas Bronckx' distant farm.

"The Middle Road is broad. A cathedral facing on it will have a commanding prospect. I am firm in my conviction that in time to come this will be the heart of the city. And my cathedral, God's cathedral, will be a heart of pulsating prayer at the city's center."

John Hughes was a man of decision. Back at his residence he pulled book after book from the library shelves to point out to Father Bayley features of this or that cathedral he had visited in Europe. His mind was already hard at work planning ways and means.

He dismissed the suggestion that he call in Patrick Keeley for preliminary consultation. Keeley, Kilkenny-born architect, had then almost a monopoly on Catholic church designing. He had been employed many times by John Hughes. That he was well on his way to establishing a record of six hundred churches of his design was no recommendation to the Archbishop for this special church of his dream. It had come to his attention, too, that on at least one occasion Keeley had designed an important church without ever visiting the site. As a result, the tower was on the upper rather than the lower side of the slightly inclined facade. No! Renwick was the better man. Renwick, John Hughes must have.

Protests came crowding from the Catholic people when he announced his decision. The site was too far out. The plans for the great building were too vainglorious. Where was the money to come from? And why Renwick, a non-Catholic; why not devout Pat Keeley? The most bitter of his opponents began to call the proposed cathedral "Hughes' Folly."

John Hughes moved on quietly with his great project.

"For the glory of Almighty God, for the honor of the Blessed and Immaculate Virgin, for the exaltation of Holy Mother Church I propose to erect a cathedral in the city of New York which may be worthy of our increasing numbers, intelligence and faith as a religious community, as a public architectural monument of the present and prospective crown of this metropolis of the American continent."

From 1853 to 1858, James Renwick worked on the plans for the vast building with his assistant, Mr. Rodrigues. Renwick was on weekly call at the Archbishop's house. Long into the night sometimes the two would bend over the spread-out blueprint rolls. They were not always in agreement. Renwick found the Archbishop a hard master but never a stubborn one when his ideas were architecturally impracticable.

John Hughes' ideas were grand. He was determined to have nothing but the best, even though the Catholic community was so much poorer than even the humblest pewholders of Grace and Trinity churches. He felt he was building not for himself, not even for his beloved people; but for their children's children in the years ahead.

The architecture was, of course, to be Gothic—of Renwick's own design but somewhat following the lines of the great German cathedral at Cologne that John Hughes had especially admired. It would be on the lines of a Latin cross with an interior length of 306 feet. It would rise to a height of 108 feet in the nave. Archbishop Hughes planned it as the largest church on the North American continent. When it was completed, it would rank as the eleventh largest church in the world.

When the plans were drawn, James Renwick offered the Archbishop two estimates: $810,000 for a building of brown free stone; $850,000 for white marble. For John Hughes there was no choice. Marble, of course.

Eventually the building contract was let to the New York firm of Hall and Joyce for $867,500. John Hughes made an interesting stipulation in the contract. While the church was building, no spirituous liquor was to be brought into the area. More than that, no workingman was to be hired who boarded at a place where liquor was sold. Inasmuch as he could, John Hughes wanted his cathedral built in the spirit of Gods craftsmen whose piety erected the great medieval churches.

With that same feeling he had decreed that the new church should have no pews. Individual pew rent by the year provided the chief financial support of most churches of the day, Catholic or Protestant. John Hughes wanted his church, like the cathedrals of Europe, to offer equal kneeling space for rich and poor— no man should have a place reserved for him above his neighbor.

He had little money on hand when he engaged the architect. He owned the property; that was about all. But as Father Thebaud was to remark in his reminiscences, John Hughes was never at a loss to raise money. No one could figure out quite how he did it, but he had that gift. In this instance he sent a personal letter to 150 of the more prosperous Catholics of the archdiocese asking for a contribution of $1,000 each.

"I shall with the help of God," he wrote to them, "bless and deposit the cornerstone on the Feast of the Assumption of this year [August 15, 1858] at precisely four o'clock in the afternoon. If, which I cannot anticipate, I shall be unsuccessful in the object of this appeal then the cornerstone shall be laid all the same and protected by an iron railing against injury until arrival of better times. I may not have the honor of seeing this cathedral consecrated but I cannot leave to my successor the honor and great privilege of seeing it begun.

"To one it is given to begin, to another to carry on and by God's blessing to make it perfect."

He ended his appeal by stating that the names of the first subscribers to the cathedral fund would have their names inscribed on a parchment to be placed in the cornerstone "where though unseen by the world they will be under the eyes of God."

His appeal was fruitful. One hundred and three people each pledged the full $1,000 he asked. Others gave lesser amounts in their means. Two non-Catholics to whom no letter had been sent gave the Archbishop $1,000 each, in their admiration for him. The Ladies of the Sacred Heart and the Sisters of Charity sent contributions. One pastor, Father James McMahon, raised his donation to $1,500. By August, 1858, the Archbishop had $73,000 actually on hand, funds enough to go ahead.

Archbishop Hughes wrote with delight to his close friend and correspondent in Rome, Father Bernard Smith, O.S.B., that he was planning the ceremonies of the cornerstone laying "on a scale which will produce a sensation in this new country."

It was so. As early as eleven o'clock in the morning on the Feast of the Assumption of that year 1858 the crowds began to assemble at the site, although the ceremonies were not to start until four. The roads from the lower city were crowded with plodding people. The Harlem Railroad had put on extra cars but not nearly enough. Horse-drawn omnibuses tangled with extra-laden carriages and rude carts all the way up the Middle Road. They had a hard time pressing through the walking throngs of the people. Sailboats and rowboats brought the Catholics of Brooklyn and Long Island into the inlets of Kips Bay and Turtle Bay or landed them on the shores of Jones's Woods. The ferries from Staten Island and New Jersey reaped a harvest. Large numbers of people came from Albany and Buffalo and the towns in between. It was estimated that the great multitude that stood and kneeled in the dusty brush extending far out from the site numbered one hundred thousand souls.

A two-story platform had been erected next to the orphan asylum. The lower level was for the brass band considered suitable for an outdoor occasion; the upper story was for the bishops and clergy and special dignitaries of the city and state. The site itself was railed off into an enclosure for fifteen thousand people. The Stars and Stripes flew at the four comers of the enclosure. A high cross banked with flowers marked the spot where the main altar would stand. In the procession that formed and marched from the rectory of the Church of St. John the Evangelist to the east were three archbishops, seven bishops and more than a hundred priests.

"Unless the Lord builds the house they labor in vain who build it," was the text that Archbishop Hughes chose for his sermon when the stone was laid. This was so much his own church that, contrary to custom, he had not invited any noted speaker to indulge in pious oratory. And although his sermon was masterly it was most of all John Hughes, their Bishop, talking to his own people, perhaps for the first time all assembled together.

He told of the building of old St. Patrick's Cathedral. "They were poor people who built it and they were very few; but their minds were as large as the cathedral which they projected and their hearts were the hearts of great men."

It was as though his vision was again reaching to the future, when it would be said that the completed new cathedral was built with the pennies of the Irish working girls. And in this instance he countered any talk about his extravagant ideas by saying that the building of the new St. Patrick's would afford the opportunity of honest work for honest men who did not want charity.

When the Atlantic telegraph cable was laid from Nova Scotia to Valencia, Ireland, Queen Victoria and President

The cornerstone of the new St. Patrick's Cathedral was laid with great ceremony.

Buchanan in August, 1858, had exchanged the first messages. John Hughes had been promised and sent the first message after that of the two rulers. First, he had planned to cable the Holy Father. Then he decided it would be more becoming to cable the Cardinal Prefect in charge of the Propaganda. He was very pleased too that he had been invited to speak at New York's civic celebration in honor of the event and to ride in a carriage in the jubilee procession "with Lord Napier and the Hon. Mr. Everett." It was a token of his pleasure that he had an account of the cable laying placed in the cathedral cornerstone.

Work on the cathedral went slowly and was finally interrupted completely by the War Between the States. John Hughes in his lifetime saw hardly more than the start of the walls, the outline of the building. But when war broke out, in his intense patriotism he had the Stars and Stripes flown from the scaffolding of the new cathedral as well as over the old St. Patrick's.

When the editor of the *Freemans Journal,* now in secular hands, attacked him for thus seemingly linking Church and State, Archbishop Hughes answered him firmly.

"I am getting old and I know this world would have gone on as well as it has if I had never lived. But I have not been able to sever my feelings and thoughts from this the only country I call mine and to which I am devoted by every prompting of my understanding and every loyal sentiment of my heart."

8

SUPPORTER OF THE UNION

One flag, one land, one heart, one hand, one Nation,
evermore!

—OLIVER WENDELL HOLMES

The growing threat of a civil war between the states had disturbed and saddened John Hughes. He personally detested slavery. In his youth he had written a poem, "The Slave," an outburst from his heart against slavery. In his later years he still thought of it as an evil but as an established fact outside his province to try and alter since no slaves were held in the area over which he had spiritual jurisdiction. He accepted the stand of the Archbishop and Bishops of the Province of Baltimore in slave-holding territory. They stressed a neutralist position and left their people to make their own judgments.

But in his deep love for the United States, he felt no issue, even slavery, was great enough to imperil the unity of the nation. The thought of secession of a state filled him with horror. He was one with Daniel Webster in believing that liberty and union were one and inseparable. On August 23, 1861, he stated his own strong views to a Southern fellow bishop, Patrick M. Lynch of Charleston, South Carolina:

"I am an advocate of the sovereignty of every State in the Union within the limits recognized and approved of by its own representative authority when the Constitution was agreed upon. . . . But the Constitution having been formed by the common consent of all the parties engaged in the framework and approval thereof, I maintain that no State has a right to secede except in the manner provided in the document itself."

The greater part of New York City Catholics had been supporters of Stephen A. Douglas in the critical prewar elections when he had opposed Abraham Lincoln. It was not only that they were stout Democrats but also because, by many public and private acts, he had personally endeared himself to them. But John Hughes was a stout supporter of Lincoln from the time of the latter's candidacy for the Presidency. It may in part have stemmed from the Archbishop's close friendship with William Seward, who became Secretary of State in Lincoln's cabinet, or from his own vision. He believed in the man and in his potential greatness. Once the war with the South began, no man in the country supported President Lincoln more loyally.

John Hughes and Secretary of State Seward were frequent correspondents. Seward often showed the Archbishop's letters to Lincoln. One letter so appealed to Lincoln that he asked Seward to have a copy of it made for him. In it Archbishop Hughes had counseled forbearance in victory and urged that the rebel leaders be treated in defeat with patience and consideration. "Conquest is not altogether by the sword. Statesmanship may have much to do with it."

Abraham Lincoln wrote John Hughes thanking him for the "kind and judicious letters" to Seward, "which he regularly allows me both the pleasure and profit of perusing."

From the shared letters, so filled with intense loyalty to the Union and wise counsels, came the idea of asking John Hughes to make a trip to Europe to present the cause of the North in a favorable light. England, because she needed cotton for her factory looms, was inclined to look favorably upon the South. It was very important that France be kept neutral in the war. John Hughes seemed the best possible choice as a spokesman for the Union.

When he reached Paris, Archbishop Hughes had some difficulty in arranging for an audience with Emperor Napoleon III. Since the Archbishop was forthright in announcing his Union sympathies, important personages shied away from him. They were not sure he spoke for the winning side.

After a few rebuffs, John Hughes took matters into his own hands. He wrote his own letter of introduction to Emperor Napoleon and asked for an audience. A letter came back at once from the Emperor and for good measure a gracious note from the Empress Eugénie expressing pleasure at the prospect of receiving him at their palace of the Tuileries.

Napoleon III bowed deeply to the Archbishop when he entered the audience chamber. The Empress swept him a deep curtsy, then moved forward gracefully to genuflect and kiss his ring. John Hughes wore the pectoral cross given him by the Belgian Queen. Empress Eugénie's darting eyes noticed its magnificence, although she herself was simply dressed and wore no jewels.

She opened the conversation, asking about his passage. "Travelers say it is but a trifle now."

"Imperial Lady, I am an old sailor. And considering the December season the passage was pleasant but a little tedious. The ship took thirteen days instead of the eleven in ordinary times."

The Emperor asked about an old American friend. "Can you tell me, Monseigneur, of General Winfield Scott? I knew him when I was in the United States."

John Hughes here saw a chance to emphasize his mission. He told the Emperor that although Scott was a Southerner he had remained faithful to the Union. Indeed, he had been in command of the Union forces until a month before when ill health had forced him to retire. Turning aside to the Empress, he said that he had had the pleasure of baptizing the general's son. She was very interested and made a slight motion to one of her attendants, who left the room.

The Emperor seemed chiefly interested in knowing how effective was the blockade of the Southern ports. He knew the economy of the Southern states was based on the sale of cotton. Could the South keep up the war if that revenue were cut off? He had heard that the blockade-runners were increasingly successful.

John Hughes had primed himself well. He was able to counter the claims made by Southern sympathizers among Napoleon's advisers. The Emperor listened to him intently and nodded his head several times in seeming agreement. The Archbishop felt very heartened.

As it came time for the audience to come to a close, there was a diversion. The Empress' attendant returned, in charge of the young Prince Imperial, who, on entering the room, ran to his mother.

She took his hand and had him make a formal bow to the American Archbishop. "Monseigneur," she said, "it is the eve of Christmas, the Feast of the Holy Infant. May I not ask you on this holy night to give your blessing to our little son?" She motioned to the five- year-old boy to kneel.

Archbishop John Hughes raised his hand and pronounced the formal Latin benediction. Then, as Eugénie, very moved, gazed at him with tears in her eyes and the Emperor bit at his mustache, he said with Irish warmth: "God bless you, my boy, and preserve you so that when you shall have grown up to be a man you may be able, under the divine benediction, to realize the good hopes that are entertained in your regard not only by your own country but by many other nations."

He commented later that the Prince Imperial was a charming boy, "a beautiful child, yet more sweet than beautiful, with the countenance of his mother."

Archbishop Hughes went on to Rome, where he took part in the ceremonies of the canonization of the twenty-six Japanese martyrs. He gloried in the magnificence of the services at St. Peter's where three hundred and twenty-three bishops, four hundred priests and a hundred thousand of the faithful heard the decree of the Holy Father elevating to the altars of the Church these saints who had given their lives for it.

But more inspiring to him were the quiet talks he had in private audience with Pope Pius IX. The American war disturbed him. It was distressful to have brother fighting against brother. He asked earnestly if it might not be possible for a European nation or nations to mediate between the North and the South. He himself would eagerly offer any help he could to bring the bloodshed of battles to an end.

Alexander Randall of Wisconsin, when he presented

his credentials as American Minister to the Papal States, spoke highly in praise of John Hughes' efforts in aid of his country. He told Pope Pius that it was "a source of regret that the United States cannot in any appropriate way testify its appreciation of such services." It was considered that he was making delicate and diplomatic reference to the wish of President Lincoln that Archbishop Hughes be considered for a cardinal's red hat.

On his return to the United States, after a visit to Ireland where he did a great deal to enlist the sympathies of the people in the Northern cause, John Hughes minimized his own part in any success of his mission. He wrote:

"I had no message to deliver . . . except the message of peace; except the message of correcting erroneous ideas as opportunity might afford me the chance of doing. I have lost no opportunity to accomplish these ends. The task was not so easy as some might have anticipated; its accomplishment has not been so successful as I could have desired. Nevertheless I trust that directly or indirectly my going abroad, in great part for the purpose of aiding the country, has not been altogether without effect."

President Lincoln and Secretary of State Seward thought that John Hughes' mission had had great effect, especially on France. The Secretary gave a banquet in Washington in the Archbishop's honor to give public governmental recognition of his services. The banquet was given on a Friday night. To Archbishop Hughes' deep pleasure at his host's thoughtfulness, fish was served as the main course. He termed it "a most delicate compliment."

This last trip abroad, unlike the others, had weakened John Hughes' health rather than restored it. His anxieties for his beloved country and his efforts to win approval for the course President Lincoln had taken had allowed him none of the relaxation of other voyages.

He came home very tired. The crippling arthritis that once he had brushed off as "a touch of rheumatism" plagued him more and more. And the kidney ailment of which he was to die was fastening itself upon him. For some years, arthritis in his hands had so dislocated the joint of his right thumb that he could no longer write his own letters and sermons. He had to dictate them to John Regan, his secretary.

He kept up the pace of his office as best he could, at times with much of his old vigor. In the week of October 16, 1862, for example, he administered the Sacrament of Confirmation to 1,400 persons. Five hundred were soldiers of Colonel Michael Corcoran's Irish Legion, in training at Camp Scott on Staten Island. At the Church of the Annunciation in Manhattanville, he confirmed another large class, and nearly seven hundred boys and girls at the old cathedral. He was touched by the sight of the little girls in their white veils and the neatly dressed boys. He saw them as living proof that his long fight to give Catholic children the benefits of a Catholic education had not been in vain.

To an assisting priest he murmured, "Look at them, bless their hearts. They show an attitude of piety which only twenty years ago it would have been vain to expect on such an occasion."

In his ailing health John Hughes was even more sickened by the rise in venom of the attacks upon himself and his people by the more fanatical New York abolitionists as the war went on.

The Irish Catholics of whom he was the shepherd had responded nobly and with enthusiasm to President Lincoln's call to arms when Fort Sumter was fired upon. Colonel Michael Corcoran had at once begun recruiting for the Sixty-ninth Regiment from among them. Although the roster for a regiment was 1,000 men, more than 1,800 eager recruits applied in person at Prince Street headquarters. Oral requests for enlistment and letters came from 3,000 others.

On April 23, 1861, the regiment attended solemn Mass at the Mott Street cathedral before marching away to win undying glory at Bull Run, Fair Oaks, Chancellorsville and Marye's Heights. At Fredericksburg, the Irish Brigade under General Thomas Francis Meagher, the men bearing green twigs in their hats, made six of the most heroic charges of the war. They were Archbishop Hughes' sons of the Eighty-eighth and Sixty-third New York Regiments as well as the Fighting Sixty-ninth. The militia company known as the Irish Rifles became the Thirty-seventh New York. The Second Battalion of Light Artillery was recruited by its four Irish captains from their fellows in New York; the battalion commander was Major Thomas O'Neill.

But all this active loyalty and positive patriotism was disregarded by New York's Republican press, which at times was fanatically abolitionist. The greater part of the Catholics of New York were Democrats and the Democratic Party was considered proslavery. Soon Horace Greeley in his *Tribune* and William Cullen Bryant, editor of the *Post,* began to attack the Irish Catholic Democrats of the city because they separated the preservation of the Union from the freeing of the slaves.

Archbishop Hughes was singled out always for especial attack, as if he had purposely rallied his people to the Democratic Party. The Archbishop had not taken partisan political sides; oddly he was, if anything, a Republican at heart. And he had been in the service of, and honored by, the Republican government then in power.

Then from Washington came a draft law. In New York military conscription was denounced both by Governor Horatio Seymour and Mayor Fernando Wood. They charged the law was unconstitutional. Thousands of less important citizens joined them in outraged opposition to conscription in a republic of a free people.

But when opposition to the military draft became widespread in the city, Horace Greeley, on July 9, 1863, published what he called "A Friendly Letter to Archbishop Hughes." It was anything but friendly. It singled out the Archbishop for being, with his people, responsible for opposition to the draft "by alliance to the Democratic party and its subsequent political successes . . . and by refusal of priests to preach the abolition and anti-slavery doctrine from their pulpits."

The Archbishop had, indeed, forbidden his priests to preach any politics from their pulpits . . . and that included abolition which had become a political issue. But he was not strongly against conscription. Upon his return from Europe in August, 1862, he had urged volunteering; but he had said he might favor a military draft if it were necessary to bring the war to a quick end. It was his hope that people would draft themselves; that there need not be coercion of free citizens. When John Mullaly, editor of the *Metropolitan Record,* which was looked upon as the Archbishop's unofficial organ, advocated open resistance to the draft in an article on March 14,1863, John Hughes immediately ordered that his own name be removed from the newspaper masthead. What he had to say to Mr. Mullaly in private we may only guess.

Opposition to the draft grew in intensity week by week.

One of the provisions of the law was that for $300 a man could buy a substitute and free himself of the obligation to bear arms. It was a law that exempted the rich and penalized the poor, cried the common citizens of New York. How could a married man needed at home to support his wife and family ever raise such a sum? Was he to leave his family destitute?

Draft drawings in New York City were to begin on Saturday, July 11, 1863. On July 9, Greeley screamed editorially at the Archbishop: "Your people for years have been and today are foremost in the degradation and abuse of this persecuted race. Have you done your duty in the premises?" He hurled the added insult that Archbishop Hughes had "imitated too generally the Priest and the Levite."

Negroes fleeing from the South had been coming into New York City in great numbers in the first two years of the war. When the men among them sought work they competed, of course, as unskilled labor with the poorer workers of the city. Indeed, in the spring of 1863, they had been used by greedy shipowners to help break a longshoreman's strike on the New York docks, then cruelly cast off in favor of white workers when the strike was settled.

There was no especial ill will between the Irish and the Negroes. Pierre Toussaint, a freeman of color, had been one of the most respected Catholics of the city, admired and even loved by his Irish co-religionists. The newer Irish immigrants knew better than Greeley what it was to be a persecuted race. They had memories not only of political enslavement but of unnecessary starvation.

However, all the humbler workers of the city, of old stock or new, looked on these newcomers doubtfully. Since the port of New York had started to boom they had known two years of full work weeks and decent wages. Now Copperheads

(Northern supporters of the South) and Confederacy agents in the city in disguise began maliciously to point out, wherever poor men gathered, that Negroes themselves were by the law exempt from the draft. They were not being forced to help free their fellows; yet white men, family men, were being asked to let their children starve while exempt Negroes took their jobs.

Egged on by Southern agitators and with a burning sense of wrong, the poor workers of the city revolted. On July 11, 1863, rioting against the draft began in the city.

The riots went on for four days of death and destruction largely affecting the Negro quarters of the city. About one thousand people were killed in the end, and hundreds injured. Not all were Negroes by any means. The hoodlums from their hidden places in the squalid city slums who joined the rioters in a greed for loot did not pick and choose among their victims.

Father Augustine Hewit of the Paulist Fathers was wounded in the head by a thrown stone when he tried to check a mob that had gathered at West 59th Street to march down Eleventh Avenue, where later they tore up horsecar tracks and burned houses indiscriminately. When St. Luke's Hospital, then at Fifth Avenue and 54th Street, was in danger from another rioting mob, it was saved by Paulist Father George Deshon. He was a former West Pointer, and the boldest in the crowd retreated before his commanding military presence. The pastor of the Catholic church on 36th Street near Second Avenue is recorded as saving from fire the buildings of Columbia College, then in the mid-city.

When another part of the mob tortured and finally killed Colonel Henry O'Brien of the Eleventh New York Volunteers on Second Avenue near 18th Street, it also stoned the elderly

Father Edward Cowery and held him back from giving Colonel O'Brien the last rites of the Church. And one of the houses in Yorkville burned by rioters was that of Provost Marshal Robert Nugent, former colonel of the Irish Sixty-ninth.

Archbishop John Hughes, crippled by his sickness, was not able to go out into the city; but he sent his priests forth to do what they could to bring peace and order. Their reports to him showed that anti-Catholic as well as anti-Negro elements were in force among the leaders of the various mobs. It was not, as first reported to him, a disorderly rabble of his own

misguided people that was responsible for the death and destruction in the city.

Even William Cullen Bryant, who at times struck out bitterly at the Archbishop and his people for what he termed their opposition to the draft, admitted in the *Post* that "In the First Ward, Irish porters and laborers formed into a guarding force and dispersed incipient riots, arrested a countryman of their own who was trying to create a disturbance, and rescued one poor Negro from the clutches of a mob."

John Hughes was reassured. He knew his people could not have so betrayed their Faith, and his own trust and

The draft riots went on for four days of death and destruction.

confidence in their devotion to law and order. The Archbishop had written Horace Greeley at once, answering his "friendly" letter of July 9. The editor, however, did not see fit to publish it until the second day of the rioting.

"In spite of Mr. Greeley's assault upon the Irish," their Archbishop wrote, "in the present disturbed condition of the city I will appeal not only to them but to all persons who love God and revere the holy Catholic religion which they profess to return to their homes with as little delay as possible."

As the rioting continued, Archbishop Hughes finally, in his anguish at what he felt were unjust aspersions against them, issued a call to his people to assemble before his Madison Avenue residence.

"To the Men of New York who are now called in many of the papers rioters!

"Men! I am not able owing to rheumatism in my limbs to visit you, but there is not a reason why you should not pay me a visit, in your whole strength. Come then tomorrow, Friday, at two o'clock to my residence, northwest corner of Madison Avenue and 36th Street. I shall have a speech prepared for you. There is abundant space for the meeting about my house. I can address you from the comer of the balcony. If I am unable to stand during its delivery you will permit me to address you sitting. My voice is much stronger than my limbs! You will not be disturbed by any exhibit of municipal or military presence. You who are Catholics, or as many of you as are, have a right to visit your Bishop without molestation."

Bryant called the Archbishop's fervent plea a shepherd's summoning of "the wolves . . . miscreants, assassins, robbers, house-burners and thieves, such a congregation of vicious and abandoned wretches as is not often got together." He urged any "sheep" among the Irish Catholics to stay away from the Archbishop's house.

But the sheep in hundreds obeyed the call of their shepherd. They assembled in a great mass of men that extended up and down Madison Avenue into the side streets. Scores of them were the sturdy citizens who had defended the cathedral and the other Catholic churches of New York City against the Nativist church burners of 1844. If many of them carried staves it was for protection as they converged on the Archbishop's house through streets where the rioters still held destructive sway.

Their hats and caps came off in a great wave as John Hughes, their Archbishop and father in God, was helped painfully by his priests to a chair on the balcony that overlooked them. He gazed for a quiet time over the great throng of sturdy, serious men come at his call, and he studied their faces. They were silent before him with the silence of deep respect. At last he spoke:

"Men of New York! They call you rioters but I cannot see a rioter's face among you. I call you men of New York. Not gentlemen because gentlemen is so threadbare a term it means nothing positive. Give me men, and I know of my own knowledge that if the city were invaded by the British or any other foreign power you would prove yourselves so. . . .

"If I could have met you anywhere else but here I would have gone, even on crutches. For I address you as your Father. . . . If you are Irishmen as your enemies say you are, I am an Irishman, too—and I am not a rioter. No, I am a man of peace. If you are Catholics, I am Catholic, too. . . .

"If when the smoke clears away the responsibility of these so-called rioters shall be thrown upon Catholics, especially Irish Catholics, and thus be centered on my heart, I wish you would tell me in what country I should have been born? But what do you say if these stories are true? Ireland? Ireland? Not Ireland, that never committed by her own sons or on her own soil, until she was oppressed, a single act of cruelty. Ireland, that has been the mother of heroes and poets but never the mother of a coward. . . .

"I shall not treat of the political question behind all this or of the rights and wrongs of the matter. I am a minister of God, a man of peace, a man who in your own trials in years past you know never deserted you. I am not a runaway Bishop in time of danger. It has been perhaps a calamity but I do not regret it that I was never conscious of fear until danger was over. Then sometimes, men, I became nervous. Now you know I could not, because the laws of God forbid it, fight for you even in a just cause. But this I can do, stand by you, advise you and die with you. . . .

"If property be destroyed, it can be replaced; but if lives are lost the departed souls cannot be recalled from the other world. . . . I counsel you not to give up your principles and convictions; but keep out of the crowds in which immortal souls are launched into eternity without a moment's notice. . . .

"Never mind these reports, these calumnies as I hope they are, against you and against me, that you are rioters and this and that. Go now to your homes with my blessing. And if you by chance as you disperse should meet a military man or a policeman, mind you now, just *look* at him!"

Raising himself painfully the old man gave his sons his blessing, and was helped indoors. There was quiet, then sudden cheering that lasted until the Archbishop appeared at the window of his study and waved gently. The streets became quietly empty. Orderly the Catholic men of New York had come at their shepherd's call. Orderly they scattered to their homes. It was the last time that most of them were to see the great eagle, who so boldly and fiercely always had defended those within the sanctuary of his nest.

9

THE GOOD FIGHT ENDED

I have fought the good fight, 1 have finished the course

—2 TIM. 4:7

ON New Years Day, 1864, a somber pall descended upon the Catholic people of New York. At the Masses on that day the priests of the city's churches had announced that Archbishop Hughes was dying. The prayers of each congregation were asked, often tearfully, for the grace of a happy death.

Men and women knelt in their pews in stunned sorrow. It was impossible that their great protector and champion could be going from them. Almost everyone knew of his crippling rheumatism, but that of their knowledge never meant death. They did not know that the speech from his balcony had been made by a man with a much graver added illness, so grave that he had said his last Mass, sadly, two months before the draft riots had begun. When word of that got about there was shame in the city. His people now knew with what cost to himself in strength and pain their shepherd had risen from his sickbed, despite the protests of his doctors, to counsel them in trust and love.

So appalled were the people that on New Year's Day and the day following they stayed prayerfully quiet in their homes. But on January 3, little knots of people began to gather early in the morning before the Madison Avenue house, kneeling on the icy ground to say the rosary. By afternoon and early evening there were throngs of people in the roadway.

Well-to-do women bent down their hoops and tucked in the hems of their crinolines to kneel with the shawled women of the poorer districts. Their men, of all conditions and classes, knelt with them. A drayman said his beads next to one of the rich and aristocratic Friendly Sons of St. Patrick, and a portly director of the Irish Emigrant Society prayed beside the humblest of his clerks.

Then in the dusk, shortly after half-past seven in the evening, a priest appeared on the first-floor balcony, his figure a dark shadow against the lighted window.

The crowd hushed instantly so that his subdued voice was clearly heard by everyone.

"Beloved brethren, of your mercy and kindness I beg of you pray for the soul of God's servant, your Archbishop and spiritual father, John Joseph Hughes. . . ."

A great mourning sigh rose from the crowd. From a huddled group of shawled old Irishwomen came the wail of the keen or death cry—the ancient Gaelic lamentation for the dead. So had the great heroes of Ireland been lamented. Thus had the women of Israel wailed and wept for the mighty Moses who had led them out of the house of bondage. It had

A priest appeared on the first-floor balcony.

been out of a bondage of their spirit and their Faith that John Hughes had led the people who mourned him most—led them to the dignity of free and equal citizens in the land he had loved so deeply.

Of them he had so proudly and gratefully testified:

"I do not think there is a diocese in Christendom in which greater unity, mutual charity, mutual cooperation in every good work, in short a more universal *esprit de corps* has prevailed than in the diocese of New York; and this extends alike to both clergy and laity."

But the feeling of sorrow and loss was not only in the hearts of his own flock. It spread through the American nation among Catholics and non-Catholics alike. For this was the man who had been so proud to render this account of his stewardship:

"My public and private life has been devoted sedulously to the duties of my station.

"I have never in my life done any action or uttered any sentiment tending to abridge a human being of all, or any, of the Rights of Conscience which I claim to enjoy myself under the American Constitution.

"I have never entered into intrigue or collusion with any political party or individual; and no political party or individual ever approached me with so insulting a proposition.

"In all my public life in New York I have done no action, uttered no sentiment, unworthy of a Christian Bishop and an American citizen.

"I have always preached that every denomination, Jews, Christians, Catholics or Protestants, of every sect and shade, were all entitled to the entire enjoyment of Freedom of Conscience without let or hindrance from any other denomination or set of denominations—no matter how small their number or how unpopular the doctrines they profess.

"I have been accustomed to pray publicly in our churches for the constituted authorities of the United States, for the welfare of my fellow citizens of all denominations, and without distinction."

Of John Hughes it could be truly said: I know mine and mine know me. So the death of the eagle was a calamity in New York City. Never in its history had there been such honor paid a clergyman of any denomination as at the funeral rites of Archbishop John Hughes. His body lay in state for two days with thousands upon thousands passing his bier in prayer.

In the custom of the day, the old St. Patrick's Cathedral was literally sheeted inside in mourning crape. A contemporary account says that "the walls and pillars were hidden under falls of black broadcoth and white merino." The pulpit and episcopal throne were draped in black "with silver tongues of flame." An arched canopy covered with black cloth "studded with tongues of flame and mounted with black and white ostrich plumes rose over the catafalque where the body of the Archbishop, in chasuble and miter, reposed."

John Hughes was in his sixty-seventh year and the thirty-eighth of his priesthood. He would be buried on the twenty-sixth anniversary of his consecration as a bishop.

An unprecedented group of eight Catholic bishops were in attendance at the solemn funeral Mass, the bishops of Albany, Buffalo, Brooklyn, Burlington, Newark, Portland, Providence and Philadelphia. Bishop John McCloskey of Albany, who had been closely associated with Archbishop Hughes and who was to become his successor, preached the eulogy. The old cathedral on Mott Street was filled with priests and nuns, civic and Army and Navy officials, and delegations of all kinds. The streets outside were massed with sorrowful men and women and children of his flock. There were even, one newspaper reporter noted with something of awe, "strangers from abroad."

In a front pew knelt his family, his seventy-year-old brother Michael and his two sisters, Mrs. Rodrigues and Sister Mary Angela, for some years Sister Superior of Mount St. Vincent's convent. They had been at his bedside when his chaplain, the Jesuit Father John McElroy, gave the dying Archbishop the last rites of the Church.

Burial was in Calvary Cemetery although at once a movement began "to have a magnificent tomb erected in the new cathedral as soon as it is finished, and there the remains will thereafter be removed as soon as means and opportunity permit the great work to be completed." Today the body of New York's first and great Archbishop does rest in the cathedral of his dreams and great vision, in a crypt below the main altar. The twin spires of St. Patrick's, in the heart of the city as he foresaw, are his great monument. They may be considered symbolic of God and Country, the two beloved treasures of John Hughes' heart.

All flags in the city were half-masted during the funeral. The Mayor of New York and the Comptroller closed all city offices for the day.

For as Mayor C. Godfrey Gunther wrote to the Common Council: "It is not that an eloquent and exalted prelate has passed away, but that in his death our country has lost an eminent citizen and pure patriot; for this we may mingle our tears with those of others bound by the most sacred ties to the departed. . . . Death has quenched the fire of his genius but has no power over his virtues."

The Common Council in answer voted to attend the funeral in a body, "with their staffs of office draped in mourning."

Yet it had been only a few short years since the Know-Nothing Party and its anti-Catholicism had threatened the city with disorders; not too many years that John Hughes had had to defend his churches against burning by the Nativists. So much, by the dignity of his person and the respect he drew to him, had John Hughes accomplished for the recognition of his people and their Church in the city of his diocesan see.

From Washington, Secretary of State Seward wrote to Vicar General William Starrs on behalf of President Abraham Lincoln that the pressure of war problems prevented him from attending the Archbishop's funeral.

"But he has, nevertheless, earnestly desired to find some practicable mode of manifesting the sorrow with which he received intelligence of that distinguished Prelate's demise, and his sympathy with his countrymen and with the religious community over which the deceased presided, in their great bereavement.

"I have, therefore, on his behalf, to request that you make known in such manner as will seem to you appropriate, that having formed the Archbishop's acquaintance in the earliest days of our country's present troubles, his counsel and advice were gladly sought and continually received by the Government on those points which his position enabled him better than others to consider.

"At a conjuncture of deep interest to the country the Archbishop, associated with others, went abroad and did the nation a service there with all the loyalty, fidelity and practical wisdom which, on so many other occasions, illustrated his great ability for administration."

On his own behalf, Secretary Seward, John Hughes' old friend, wrote Vicar General Starrs of "the respect and affection which I have so long cherished towards him as a faithful friend, a pious prelate, a loyal patriot, a great and a good man."

It remained for Horatio Seymour, Governor of the State of New York to use words of prophecy now come true:

"The life-long labors of the late Archbishop will tell for a long time upon the literature, the religion, and the charitable institutions of our land. In a few years the city of New York will be adorned by a magnificent Cathedral, the broad foundations of which were laid under his supervision and care. So, too, in the future, will the interests of learning, religion and charity be built upon the groundworks which he has established during his long and laborious life."

John Hughes would have liked best the comment of a later-day historian: "All that he did he did with the greater good of his country in his mind and in his heart." The eagle of St. John was the symbol of his patron in the Church; the American eagle that of his country. He cherished the things for which they both stood beyond most men.

ABOUT THE AUTHOR

Doran Hurley was born in Fall River, Massachusetts, where he received his elementary and high school education. After attending Providence College for several years, he completed work for his degree at Brown University. In the early days of radio, he was an announcer and station manager—it was his voice that announced that Charles Lindbergh had landed safely in France after his historic flight across the Atlantic Ocean.

Later turning to writing, Mr. Hurley produced several books, among them *Monsignor, The Old Parish, Herself: Mrs. Patrick Crowley,* and *Says Mrs. Crowley, Says She.* After serving in the Armored Force and in Public Relations during World War II, he engaged in newspaper work, and now as a free-lance writer living in New York, he contributes to magazines such as *The Magnificat, The Catholic World, St. Joseph Magazine, America,* and *The Sign.*

www.ingramcontent.com/pod-product-compliance
Lightning Source LLC
LaVergne TN
LVHW091152080426
835509LV00006B/650